MYSTICISM IN
ENGLISH LITERATURE

MYSTICISM
IN ENGLISH
LITERATURE

BY

CAROLINE F. E. SPURGEON

KENNIKAT PRESS
Port Washington, N. Y./London

" Many are the thyrsus-bearers, but few are the mystics "

Pʜᴁᴅᴏ

MYSTICISM IN ENGLISH LITERATURE

First published in 1913
Reissued in 1970 by Kennikat Press
Library of Congress Catalog Card No: 74-105838
ISBN 0-8046-0981-0

Manufactured by Taylor Publishing Company   Dallas, Texas

NOTE

THE variety of applications of the term " mysticism " has forced me to restrict myself here to a discussion of that philosophical type of mysticism which concerns itself with questions of ultimate reality. My aim, too, has been to consider this subject in connection with great English writers. I have had, therefore, to exclude, with regret, the literature of America, so rich in mystical thought.

I wish to thank Mr John Murray for kind permission to make use of an article of mine which appeared in the *Quarterly Review*, and also Dr Ward and Mr Waller for similar permission with regard to certain passages in a chapter of the *Cambridge History of English Literature*, vol. ix.

I am also indebted to Mr Bertram Dobell, Messrs Longmans, Green, Mrs Coventry Patmore and Mr Francis Meynell for most kindly allowing me to quote from the works respectively of Thomas Traherne, Richard Jefferies, Coventry Patmore, and Francis Thompson.

C. F. E. S.

April 1913.

CONTENTS

MYSTICISM IN
ENGLISH LITERATURE

CHAPTER I

INTRODUCTION

MYSTICISM is a term so irresponsibly applied in
English that it has become the first duty of those
who use it to explain what they mean by it. The
Concise Oxford Dictionary (1911), after defining a
mystic as " one who believes in spiritual apprehension of truths beyond the understanding," adds,
" whence *mysticism* (n.) (often contempt)." Whatever may be the precise force of the remark in
brackets, it is unquestionably true that mysticism
is often used in a semi-contemptuous way to denote
vaguely any kind of occultism or spiritualism, or
any specially curious or fantastic views about God
and the universe.

The word itself was originally taken over by the
Neo-platonists from the Greek mysteries, where
the name of μύστης, given to the initiate, probably
arose from the fact that he was one who was gaining
a knowledge of divine things about which he must

1

keep his mouth shut ($\mu\acute{v}\omega=$ close lips or eyes). Hence the association of secrecy or "mystery" which still clings round the word.

Two facts in connection with mysticism are undeniable, whatever it may be, and whatever part it is destined to play in the development of thought and of knowledge. In the first place, it is the leading characteristic of some of the greatest thinkers of the world—of the founders of the Eastern religions, of Plato and Plotinus, of Eckhart and Bruno, of Spinoza, Goethe, and Hegel. Secondly, no one has ever been a lukewarm, an indifferent, or an unhappy mystic. If a man has this particular temperament, his mysticism is the very centre of his being : it is the flame which feeds his whole life ; and he is intensely and supremely happy just so far as he is steeped in it.

Mysticism is, in truth, a temper rather than a doctrine, an atmosphere rather than a system of philosophy. Various mystical thinkers have contributed fresh aspects of Truth as they saw her, for they have caught glimpses of her face at different angles, transfigured by diverse emotions, so that their testimony, and in some respects their views, are dissimilar to the point of contradiction. Wordsworth, for instance, gained his revelation of divinity through Nature, and through Nature alone ; whereas to Blake " Nature was a hindrance," and Imagination the only reality. But all alike agree in one respect, in one passionate assertion, and this is that unity underlies diversity. This, their starting-point and their goal, is the basic fact of mysticism, which, in its widest sense, may be described as an attitude of mind founded upon an intuitive or experienced conviction of unity, of oneness, of alikeness in all things. From this source springs all mystical thought, and the mystic, of whatever age or country, would say in the words of Krishna—

> There is true knowledge. Learn thou it is this :
> To see one changeless Life in all the Lives,
> And in the Separate, One Inseparable.
>
> *The Bhagavad-Gîtâ*, Book 18.

This fundamental belief in unity leads naturally to the further belief that all things about us are but forms or manifestations of the one divine life, and that these phenomena are fleeting and impermanent, although the spirit which informs them is immortal and endures. In other words, it leads to the belief that " the Ideal is the only Real."

Further, if unity lies at the root of things, man must have some share of the nature of God, for he is a spark of the Divine. Consequently, man is capable of knowing God through this godlike part of his own nature, that is, through his soul or spirit. For the mystic believes that as the intellect is given us to apprehend material things, so the spirit is given us to apprehend spiritual things, and that to disregard the spirit in spiritual matters, and to trust to reason is as foolish as if a carpenter, about to begin a piece of work, were deliberately to reject his keenest and sharpest tool. The methods of mental and spiritual knowledge are entirely different. For we know a thing mentally by looking at it from outside, by comparing it with other things, by analysing and defining it, whereas we can know a thing spiritually only by becoming it. We must *be* the thing itself, and not merely talk about it or look at it. We must be in love if we are to know what love is ; we must be musicians if we are to know what music is ; we must be godlike if we are to know what God is. For, in Porphyry's words : " Like is known only by like, and the condition of all knowledge is that the subject should become like to the object." So that to the mystic, whether he be philosopher, poet, artist, or priest, the aim of life is to become like God, and thus to attain to union with the Divine. Hence, for him, life is a continual advance, a ceaseless aspiration ; and reality or truth is to the seeker after it a vista ever expanding and charged with ever deeper meaning. John Smith, the Cambridge Platonist, has summed up the mystic position and desire in one brief sentence, when he says, " Such as men themselves

are, such will God Himself seem to them to be."
For, as it takes two to communicate the truth, one
to speak and one to hear, so our knowledge of God
is precisely and accurately limited by our capacity
to receive Him. " Simple people," says Eckhart,
" conceive that we are to see God as if He stood
on that side and we on this. It is not so : God
and I are one in the act of my perceiving Him."

This sense of unity leads to another belief,
though it is one not always consistently or definitely
stated by all mystics. It is implied by Plato when
he says, " All knowledge is recollection." This is
the belief in pre-existence or persistent life, the
belief that our souls are immortal, and no more
came into existence when we were born than
they will cease to exist when our bodies disintegrate.
The idea is familiar in Wordsworth's *Ode on the
Intimations of Immortality*.

Finally, the mystic holds these views because he
has lived through an experience which has forced
him to this attitude of mind. This is his distin-
guishing mark, this is what differentiates him alike
from the theologian, the logician, the rationalist
philosopher, and the man of science, for he bases
his belief, not on revelation, logic, reason, or demon-
strated facts, but on *feeling*, on intuitive inner
knowledge.

He has felt, he has seen, and he is therefore

convinced ; but his experience does not convince any one else. The mystic is somewhat in the position of a man who, in a world of blind men, has suddenly been granted sight, and who, gazing at the sunrise, and overwhelmed by the glory of it, tries, however falteringly, to convey to his fellows what he sees. They, naturally, would be sceptical about it, and would be inclined to say that he is talking foolishly and incoherently. But the simile is not altogether parallel. There is this difference. The mystic is not alone ; all through the ages we have the testimony of men and women to whom this vision has been granted, and the record of what they have seen is amazingly similar, considering the disparity of personality and circumstances. And further, the world is not peopled with totally blind men. The mystics would never hold the audience they do hold, were it not that the vast majority of people have in themselves what William James has called a " mystical germ " which makes response to their message.

James's description of his own position in this matter, and his feeling for a " Beyond," is one to which numberless " unmystical " people would subscribe. He compares it to a tune that is always singing in the back of his mind, but which he can never identify nor whistle nor get rid of. " It is," he says, " very vague, and impossible to describe or put into words . . . Especially at times of moral crisis it comes to me, as the sense of an unknown something backing me up. It is most indefinite, to be sure, and rather faint. And yet I know that if it should cease there would be a great hush, a great void in my life." [1]

This sensation, which many people experience vaguely and intermittently, and especially at times of emotional exaltation, would seem to be the first glimmerings of that secret power which, with the mystics, is so finely developed and sustained that it becomes their definite faculty of vision. We have as yet no recognised name for this faculty, and it has been variously called " transcendental feeling," " imagination," " mystic reason," " cosmic consciousness," " divine sagacity," " ecstasy," or " vision," all these meaning the same thing. But although it lacks a common name, we have ample testimony to its existence, the testimony of the greatest teachers, philosophers, and poets of the world, who describe to us in strangely similar language—

> That serene and blessed mood
> In which . . . the breath of this corporeal frame,
> And even the motion of our human blood,
> Almost suspended, we are laid asleep
> In body, and become a living soul :
> While with an eye made quiet by the power

---

[1] "The Religious Philosophy of William James," by J. B. Pratt, *Hibbert Journal*, Oct. 1911, p. 232.

> Of harmony, and the deep power of joy,
> We see into the life of things.
>
> *Tintern Abbey.*

" Harmony " and " Joy," it may be noted, are the two words used most constantly by those who have experienced this vision.

The mystic reverses the ordinary methods of reasoning : he must believe before he can know. As it is put in the *Theologia Germanica*, " He who would know before he believeth cometh never to true knowledge." Just as the sense of touch is not the faculty concerned with realising the beauty of the sunrise, so the intellect is not the faculty concerned with spiritual knowledge, and ordinary intellectual methods of proof, therefore, or of argument, the mystic holds, are powerless and futile before these questions ; for, in the words of Tennyson's Ancient Sage—

> Thou canst not prove the Nameless, O my son,
> Nor canst thou prove the world thou movest in :
> Thou canst not prove that thou art body alone,
> Nor canst thou prove that thou art spirit alone,
> Nor canst thou prove that thou art both in one :
> Thou canst not prove thou art immortal, no,
> Nor yet that thou art mortal—nay, my son,
> Thou canst not prove that I who speak with thee
> Am not thyself in converse with thyself,
> For nothing worthy proving can be proven,
> Nor yet disproven.

Symbolism is of immense importance in mysticism ;

indeed, symbolism and mythology are, as it were, the language of the mystic. This necessity for symbolism is an integral part of the belief in unity; for the essence of true symbolism rests on the belief that all things in Nature have something in common, something in which they are really alike. In order to be a true symbol, a thing must be partly the same as that which it symbolises. Thus, human love is symbolic of divine love, because, although working in another plane, it is governed by similar laws and gives rise to similar results; or falling leaves are a symbol of human mortality, because they are examples of the same law which operates through all manifestation of life. Some of the most illuminating notes ever written on the nature of symbolism are in a short paper by R. L. Nettleship,[1] where he defines true mysticism as " the consciousness that everything which we experience, every ' fact,' is an element and only an element in ' the fact '; i.e. that, in being what it is, it is significant or symbolic of more." In short, every truth apprehended by finite intelligence must by its very nature only be the husk of a deeper truth, and by the aid of symbolism we are often enabled to catch a reflection of a truth which we are not capable of apprehending in any other way.

[1] On "Spirit," in *Philosophical Remains of R. L. Nettleship*, ed. A. C. Bradley, 1901, pp. 23-32.

Nettleship points out, for instance, that bread can only be itself, can only *be* food, by entering into something else, assimilating and being assimilated, and that the more it loses itself (what it began by being) the more it " finds itself " (what it is intended to be). If we follow carefully the analysis Nettleship makes of the action of bread in the physical world, we can see that to the man of mystic temper it throws more light than do volumes of sermons on what seems sometimes a hard saying, and what is at the same time the ultimate mystical counsel, " He that loveth his life shall lose it."

It is worth while, in this connection, to ponder the constant use Christ makes of nature symbolism, drawing the attention of His hearers to the analogies in the law we see working around us to the same law working in the spiritual world. The yearly harvest, the sower and his seed, the leaven in the loaf, the grain of mustard-seed, the lilies of the field, the action of fire, worms, moth, rust, bread, wine, and water, the mystery of the wind, unseen and yet felt— each one of these is shown to contain and exemplify a great and abiding truth.

This is the attitude, these are the things, which lie at the heart of mysticism. In the light of this, nothing in the world is trivial, nothing is unimportant, nothing is common or unclean. It is the feeling that Blake has crystallised in the lines :

> To see a world in a grain of sand
> And a Heaven in a wild flower,
> Hold Infinity in the palm of your hand
> And Eternity in an hour.

The true mystic then, in the full sense of the term, is one who *knows* there is unity under diversity at the centre of all existence, and he knows it by the most perfect of all tests for the person concerned, because he has felt it. True mysticism—and this cannot be over-emphasised—is an experience and a life. It is an experimental science, and, as Patmore has said, it is as incommunicable to those who have not experienced it as is the odour of a violet to those who have never smelt one. In its highest consummation it is the supreme adventure of the soul : to use the matchless words of Plotinus, it is " the flight of the Alone to the Alone."

As distinguished, therefore, from the mystical thinker or philosopher, the practical mystic has direct knowledge of a truth which for him is absolute. He consequently has invariably acted upon this knowledge, as inevitably as the blind man to whom sight had been granted would make use of his eyes.

Among English writers and poets the only two who fulfil this strict definition of a mystic are Wordsworth and Blake. But we are not here concerned primarily with a study of those great souls who are mystics in the full and supreme sense of the word. For an examination of their lives and vision Evelyn Underhill's valuable book should be consulted. Our object is to examine very briefly the chief English writers—men of letters and poets—whose inmost principle is rooted in mysticism, or whose work is on the whole so permeated by mystical thought that their attitude of mind is not fully to be understood apart from it.

Naturally it is with the poets we find the most complete and continuous expression of mystical thought and inspiration. Naturally, because it has ever been the habit of the English race to clothe their profoundest thought and their highest aspiration in poetic form. We do not possess a Plato, a Kant, or a Descartes, but we have Shakespeare and Wordsworth and Browning. And further, as the essence of mysticism is to believe that everything we see and know is symbolic of something greater, mysticism is on one side the poetry of life. For poetry, also, consists in finding resemblances, and universalises the particulars with which it deals. Hence the utterances of the poets on mystical philosophy are peculiarly valuable. The philosopher approaches philosophy directly, the poet obliquely ; but the indirect teaching of a poet touches us more profoundly than the direct lesson of a moral treatise, because the latter appeals principally to

our reason, whereas the poet touches our " transcendental feeling."

So it is that mysticism underlies the thought of
most of our great poets, of nearly all our greatest
poets, if we except Chaucer, Dryden, Pope, and Byron.
Shakespeare must be left on one side, first, because
the dramatic form does not lend itself to the expression of mystical feeling, and secondly, because even
in the poems there is little real mysticism, though
there is much of the fashionable Platonism. Shakespeare is metaphysical rather than mystical, the
difference being, roughly, that the metaphysician
seeks to know the beginnings or causes of things,
whereas the mystic feels he knows the end of
things, that all nature is leading up to union with
the One.

We shall find that mystical thought, and the
mystical attitude, are curiously persistent in English
literature, and that although it seems out of keeping
with our " John Bull " character, the English race
has a marked tendency towards mysticism. What
we do find lacking in England is the purely philosophical and speculative spirit of the detached and
unprejudiced seeker after truth. The English
mind is anti-speculative; it cares little for metaphysics; it prefers theology and a given authority.
English mystics have, as a rule, dealt little with
the theoretical side of mysticism, the aspect for

instance with which Plotinus largely deals. They
have been mainly practical mystics, such as William
Law. Those of the poets who have consciously
had a system and desired to impart it, have done
so from the practical point of view, urging, like
Wordsworth, the importance of contemplation and
meditation, or, like Blake, the value of cultivating
the imagination ; and in both cases enforcing the
necessity of cleansing the inner life, if we are to
become conscious of our divine nature and our
great heritage.

For the sake of clearness, this thought may
first be traced very briefly as it appears chrono-
logically ; it will, however, be considered in detail,
not in order of time, but according to the special
aspect of Being through which the writer felt most
in touch with the divine life. For mystics, unlike
other thinkers, scientific or philosophical, have
little chronological development, since " mystic
truths can neither age nor die." So much is this
the case that passages of Plotinus and Tennyson,
of Boehme and Law, of Eckhart and Browning,
may be placed side by side and be scarcely dis-
tinguishable in thought. Yet, as the race evolves,
certain avenues of sensation seem to become more
widely opened up. This is noticeable with regard
to Nature. Love, Beauty, Wisdom, and Devotion,
these have been well-trodden paths to the One

ever since the days of Plato and Plotinus ; but, with the great exception of St Francis of Assisi and his immediate followers, we have to wait for more modern times before we find the intense feeling of the Divinity in Nature which we associate with the name of Wordsworth. It is in the emphasis of this aspect of the mystic vision that English writers are supreme. Henry Vaughan, Wordsworth, Browning, Richard Jefferies, Francis Thompson, and a host of other poet-seers have crystallised in immortal words this illuminated vision of the world.

The thought which has been described as mystical has its roots in the East, in the great Oriental religions. The mysterious " secret " taught by the Upanishads is that the soul or spiritual consciousness is the only source of true knowledge. The Hindu calls the soul the " seer " or the " knower," and thinks of it as a great eye in the centre of his being, which, if he concentrates his attention upon it, is able to look outwards and to gaze upon Reality. The soul is capable of this because in essence it is one with Brahman, the universal soul. The apparent separation is an illusion wrought by matter. Hence, to the Hindu, matter is an obstruction and a deception, and the Eastern mystic despises and rejects and subdues all that is material, and bends all his faculties on realising his spiritual consciousness, and dwelling in that.

This type of thought certainly existed to some extent in both Greece and Egypt before the Christian era. Much of Plato's thought is mystical in essence, and that which he points out to be the motive force of the philosophic mind is also the motive force of the mystic, namely, the element of attraction, and so of love towards the thing which is akin to him. The illustration of the dog being philosophic because he is angry with a stranger but welcomes his friend,[1] though at first it may seem, like many of Plato's illustrations, far-fetched or fanciful, in truth goes to the very root of his idea. Familiarity, akinness, is the basis of attraction and affection. The desire of wisdom, or the love of beauty, is therefore nothing but the yearning of the soul to join itself to what is akin to it. This is the leading conception of the two great mystical dialogues, the Symposium and the Phædrus. In the former, Socrates, in the words of the stranger prophetess Diotima, traces the path along which the soul must travel, and points out the steps of the ladder to be climbed in order to attain to union with the Divine. From beauty of form and body we rise to beauty of mind and spirit, and so to the Beauty of God Himself.

He who under the influence of true love rising upward from these begins to see that beauty, is not far from the end. And the

---

[1] *Republic*, ii. 376.

true order of going or being led by another to the things of love, is
to use the beauties of earth as steps along which he mounts upwards
for the sake of that other beauty, going from one to two, and from
two to all fair forms, and from fair forms to fair practices, and from
fair practices to fair notions, until from fair notions he arrives at
the notion of absolute beauty, and at last knows what the essence of
beauty is.   This . . . is that life above all others which man should
live, in the contemplation of beauty absolute.[1]

That is a passage whose music re-echoes through
many pages of English literature, especially in the
poems of Spenser, Shelley, and Keats.

Plato may therefore be regarded as the source of
speculative mysticism in Europe, but it is Plotinus,
his disciple, the Neo-platonist, who is the father of
European mysticism in its full sense, practical as
well as speculative, and who is also its most profound exponent.   Plotinus (A.D. 204-270), who was
an Egyptian by birth, lived and studied under
Ammonius Sakkas in Alexandria at a time when it
was the centre of the intellectual world, seething
with speculation and schools, teachers and philo-
sophies of all kinds, Platonic and Oriental, Egyptian
and Christian.   Later, from the age of forty, he
taught in Rome, where he was surrounded by
many eager adherents.   He drew the form of his
thought both from Plato and from Hermetic
philosophy (his conception of Emanation), but its
real inspiration was his own experience, for his

[1] *Symposium*, 211, 212.

biographer Porphyry has recorded that during the six years he lived with Plotinus the latter attained four times to ecstatic union with " the One." Plotinus combined, in unusual measure, the intellect of the metaphysician with the temperament of the great psychic, so that he was able to analyse with the most precise dialectic, experiences which in most cases paralyse the tongue and blind the discursive reason. His sixth Ennead, " On the Good or the One," is one of the great philosophic treatises of the world, and it sums up in matchless words the whole mystic position and experience. There are two statements in it which contain the centre of the writer's thought. " God is not external to any one, but is present in all things, though they are ignorant that he is so." " God is not in a certain place, but wherever anything is able to come into contact with him there he is present " (*Enn*. vi. 9, §§ 4, 7). It is because of our ignorance of the indwelling of God that our life is discordant, for it is clashing with its own inmost principle. We do not know ourselves. If we did, we would know that the way home to God lies within ourselves. " A soul that knows itself must know that the proper direction of its energy is not outwards in a straight line, but round a centre which is within it " (*Enn*. vi. 9, § 8).

The whole Universe is one vast Organism (*Enn*.

ix. 4, §§ 32, 45), and the Heart of God, the source of all life, is at the centre, in which all finite things have their being, and to which they must flow back; for there is in this Organism, so Plotinus conceives, a double circulatory movement, an eternal out-breathing and in-breathing, the way down and the way up. The way down is the out-going of the undivided " One " towards manifestation. From Him there flows out a succession of emanations. The first of these is the " Nous " or Over-Mind of the Universe, God as thought. The " Mind " in turn throws out an image, the third Principle in this Trinity, the Soul of all things. This, like the " Nous," is immaterial, but it can act on matter. It is the link between man and God, for it has a lower and a higher side. The lower side *desires* a body and so creates it, but it is not wholly incarnate in it, for, as Plotinus says, " the soul always leaves something of itself above."

From this World Soul proceed the individual souls of men, and they partake of its nature. Its nature is triple, the animal or sensual soul, closely bound to the body, the logical reasoning human soul, and the intellectual soul, which is one with the Divine Mind, from whence it comes and of which it is an image.

Souls have forgotten their divine origin because at first they were so delighted with their liberty

and surroundings (like children let loose from
their parents, says Plotinus), that they ran away
in a direction as far as possible from their source.
They thus became clogged with the joys and dis-
tractions of this lower life, which can never satisfy
them, and they are ignorant of their own true
nature and essence. In order to return home,
the soul has to retrace the path along which she
came, and the first step is to get to know herself,
and so to know God. (See *Enn.* vi. 9, § 7.) Thus
only can she be restored to the central unity of the
universal soul. This first stage on the upward
path is the purgative life, which includes all the
civic and social virtues, gained through general
purification, self-discipline, and balance, with, at
the same time, a gradual attainment of detachment
from the things of sense, and a desire for the things
of the spirit.

The next step is to rise up to mind (*Enn.* v.
1, § 3) to the world of pure thought, the highest
unity possible to a self-conscious being. This is
often called the illuminative life, and it might be
summed up as concentration of all the faculties
—will, intellect, feeling—upon God. And lastly
comes the unitive life, which is contemplation,
the intense desire of the soul for union with God,
the momentary foretaste of which has been experienced by many of the mystics. This last stage

of the journey home, the supreme Adventure, the ascension to the One above thought, this cannot be spoken of or explained in words, for it is a state beyond words, it is " a mode of vision which is ecstasy." When the soul attains to this state, the One suddenly appears, " with nothing between," " and they are no more two but one ; and the soul is no more conscious of the body or of whether she lives or is a human being or an essence ; she knows only that she has what she desired, that she is where no deception can come, and that she would not exchange her bliss for the whole of Heaven itself " (paraphrased from *Enn.* vi. 7, § 24).

The influence of Plotinus upon later Christian mysticism was immense, though mainly indirect, through the writings of two of his spiritual disciples, St Augustine (354-450), and the unknown writer, probably of the early sixth century, possibly a Syrian monk, who ascribes his works to Dionysius the Areopagite, the friend of St Paul. The works of " Dionysius " were translated from Greek into Latin by the great Irish philosopher and scholar, John Scotus Erigena (Eriugena), and in that form they widely influenced later mediæval mysticism.

The fusion of Eastern mysticism with Christianity finally brought about the great change which constitutes the difference between Eastern and Western mysticism, a change already foreshadowed in Plato, for it was in part the natural outcome of the Greek delight in material beauty, but finally consummated by the teachings of the Christian faith. / Eastern thought was pure soul-consciousness, its teaching was to annihilate the flesh, to deny its reality, to look within, and so to gain enlightenment. Christianity, on the other hand, was centred in the doctrine of the Incarnation, in the mystery of God the Father revealing Himself in human form. Hence the human body, human love and relationships became sanctified, became indeed a means of revelation of the divine, and the mystic no longer turned his thoughts wholly inwards, but also outwards and upwards, to the Father who loved him and to the Son who had died for him. Thus, in the West, mystical thought has ever recognised the deep symbolism and sacredness of all that is human and natural, of human love, of the human intellect, and of the natural world. All those things which to the Eastern thinker are but an obstruction and a veil, to the Western have become the very means of spiritual ascent.[1] The ultimate goal of the Eastern mystic is summed up in his assertion,

[1] This distinction between East and West holds good on the whole, although on the one side we find the heretical Brahmin followers of *Bhakti*, and Ramananda and his great disciple, Kabir, who taught that man was the supreme manifestation of God; and on the other, occasional lapses into Quietism and repudiation of the body. See *The Mystic Way*, by E. Underhill, pp. 22-28.

" I am Brahman," whereas the Western mystic
believes that " he who sees the Infinite in all things,
sees God."

In the twelfth and thirteenth centuries the
mystical tradition was carried on in France by
St Bernard (1091-1153), the Abbot of Clairvaux,
and the Scotch or Irish Richard of the Abbey
of St Victor at Paris, and in Italy, among ·many
others, by St Bonaventura (1221-1274), a close
student of Dionysius, and these three form the
chief direct influences on our earliest English
mystics.

England shares to the full in the wave of mystical
experience, thought, and teaching which swept
over Europe in the fourteenth and early fifteenth
centuries, and at first the mystical literature of
England, as also of France, Germany, Italy, and
Sweden, is purely religious or devotional in type,
prose treatises for the most part containing practical
instruction for the inner life, written by hermits,
priests, and " anchoresses." In the fourteenth
century we have a group of such writers of great
power and beauty, and in the work of Richard
Rolle, Walter Hilton, Julian of Norwich, and the
author of the *Cloud of Unknowing*, we have a body
of writings dealing with the inner life, and the steps
of purification, contemplation, and ecstatic union
which throb with life and devotional fervour.

From the time of Julian of Norwich, who was still alive in 1413, we find practically no literature of a mystical type until we come to Spenser's *Hymns* (1596), and these embody a Platonism reached largely through the intellect, and not a mystic experience. It would seem at first sight as if these hymns, or at any rate the two later ones in honour of Heavenly Love and of Heavenly Beauty, should rank as some of the finest mystical verse in English. Yet this is not the case. They are saturated with the spirit of Plato, and they express in musical form the lofty ideas of the *Symposium* and the *Phœdrus* : that beauty, more nearly than any other earthly thing, resembles its heavenly prototype, and that therefore the sight of it kindles love, which is the excitement and rapture aroused in the soul by the remembrance of that divine beauty which once it knew. And Spenser, following Plato, traces the stages of ascent traversed by the lover of beauty, until he is caught up into union with God Himself. Yet, notwithstanding their melody and their Platonic doctrine, the note of the real mystic is wanting in the *Hymns*, the note of him who writes of these things because he knows them.

It would take some space to support this view in detail. Any one desirous of testing it might read the account of transport of the soul when rapt into union with the One as given by Plotinus

(*Enn.* vi. 9, § 10), and compare it with Spenser's description of a similar experience (*An Hymne of Heavenly Beautie*, ll. 253-273). Despite their poetic melody, Spenser's words sound poor and trivial. Instead of preferring to dwell on the unutterable ecstasy, contentment, and bliss of the experience, he is far more anxious to emphasise the fact that " all that pleased earst now seemes to paine."

The contradictory nature of his belief is also arresting. In the early part of the *Hymne of Heavenly Beautie*, in speaking of the glory of God which is so dazzling that angels themselves may not endure His sight, he says, as Plato does,

> The meanes, therefore, which unto us is lent
> Him to behold, is on his workes to looke,
> Which he hath made in beauty excellent.

This is the view of the true mystic, that God may be seen in all His works, by the eye which is itself purified. Yet, in the last stanza of this beautiful Hymn, this is how Spenser views the joy of the union of the soul with its source, when it looks

> at last up to that Soveraine Light,
> From whose pure beams al perfect beauty springs,
> That kindleth love in every godly spright
> Even the love of God ; *which loathing brings*
> *Of this vile world and these gay-seeming things.*

This is not the voice of the mystic. It is the voice

of the Puritan, who is also an artist, who shrinks from earthly beauty because it attracts him, who fears it, and tries to despise it. In truth, the dominating feature in Spenser's poetry is a curious blending of Puritanism of spirit with the Platonic mind.

In the seventeenth century, however, England is peculiarly rich in writers steeped in mystical thought.

First come the Quakers, headed by George Fox. This rediscovery and assertion of the mystical element in religion gave rise to a great deal of writing, much of it very interesting to the student of religious thought. Among the *Journals* of the early Quakers, and especially that of George Fox, there are passages which charm us with their sincerity, quaintness, and pure flame of enthusiasm, but these works cannot as a whole be ranked as literature. Then we have the little group of Cambridge Platonists, Henry More, John Smith, Benjamin Whichcote, and John Norris of Bemerton. These are all Platonic philosophers, and among their writings, and especially in those of John Norris, are many passages of mystical thought clothed in noble prose. Henry More, who is also a poet, is in character a typical mystic, serene, buoyant, and so spiritually happy that, as he told a friend, he was sometimes " almost mad with pleasure." His poetical faculty is, however, entirely

subordinated to his philosophy, and the larger
portion of his work consists of passages from the
Enneads of Plotinus turned into rather obscure verse.
So that he is not a poet and artist who, working
in the sphere of the imagination, can directly present
to us mystical thoughts and ideas, but rather a
mystic philosopher who has versified some of his
discourses. At this time also many of the " metaphysical poets " are mystical in much of their
thought. Chief among these is John Donne, and
we may also include Henry Vaughan, Traherne,
Crashaw, and George Herbert.

Bunyan might at first sight appear to have
many of the characteristics of the mystic, for he
had certain very intense psychic experiences which
are of the nature of a direct revelation of God to
the soul ; and in his vivid religious autobiography,
Grace Abounding, he records sensations which are
akin to those felt by Rolle, Julian, and many others.
But although psychically akin, he is in truth widely
separated from the mystics in spirit and temperament and belief. He is a Puritan, overwhelmed
with a sense of sin, the horrors of punishment in
hell, and the wrath of an outside Creator and Judge,
and his desire is aimed at escape from this wrath
through " election " and God's grace. But he is
a Puritan endowed with a psychopathic temperament, sensitive to the point of disease and gifted

with an abnormally high visualising power. Hence his resemblance to the mystics, which is a resemblance of psychical temperament and not of spiritual attitude.

In the eighteenth century the names of William Law and William Blake shine out like stars against a dark firmament of "rationalism" and unbelief. Their writings form a remarkable contrast to the prevailing spirit of the time. Law expresses in clear and pointed prose the main teachings of the German seer Jacob Boehme;[1] whereas Blake sees visions and has knowledge which he strives to condense into forms of picture and verse which may be understood of men. The influence of Boehme in the eighteenth and nineteenth centuries is very far-reaching. In addition to completely subjugating the strong intellect of Law, he profoundly influenced Blake. He also affected Thomas Erskine of Linlathen, and through him, Carlyle, J. W. Farquhar, F. D. Maurice, and others. Hegel, Schelling, and Schlegel are alike indebted to him, and through them, through his French disciple St Martin, and through Coleridge—who was much attracted to him—some of his root-ideas returned again to England in the nineteenth century, thus preparing the way for a better understanding of mystical thought. The Swedish seer Emmanuel

[1] For an account of Boehme's philosophy, see pp. 91-93 below.

Swedenborg (1688-1772) was another strong influence in the later eighteenth and the nineteenth centuries. Swedenborg in some ways is curiously material, at any rate in expression, and in one point at least he differs from other mystics. That is, he does not seem to believe that man has within him a spark of the divine essence, but rather that he is an organ that reflects the divine life. He is a recipient of life, but not a part of life itself. God is thought of as a light or sun outside, from which spiritual heat and light (=love and wisdom) flow into men. But, apart from this important difference, Swedenborg's thought and teaching are entirely mystical. He believes in the substantial reality of spiritual things, and that the most essential part of a person's nature, that which he carries with him into the spiritual world, is his love. He teaches that heaven is not a place, but a condition, that there is no question of outside rewards or punishments, and man makes his own heaven or hell ; for, as Patmore pointedly expresses it—

> Ice-cold seems heaven's noble glow
> To spirits whose vital heat is hell.

He insists that Space and Time belong only to physical life, and when men pass into the spiritual world that love is the bond of union, and thought or "state" makes presence, for thought is act.

He holds that instinct is spiritual in origin ; and the principle of his science of correspondences is based on the belief that everything outward and visible corresponds to some invisible entity which is its inward and spiritual cause. This is the view echoed by Mrs Browning more than once in *Aurora Leigh*—

> There's not a flower of spring,
> That dies in June, but vaunts itself allied
> By issue and symbol, by significance
> And correspondence, to that spirit-world
> Outside the limits of our space and time,
> Whereto we are bound.

In all this and much more, Swedenborg's thought is mystical, and it has had a quite unsuspected amount of influence in England, and it is diffused through a good deal of English literature.

Blake knew some at least of Swedenborg's books well ; two of his friends, C. A. Tulk and Flaxman, were devoted Swedenborgians, and he told Tulk that he had two different states, one in which he liked Swedenborg's writings, and one in which he disliked them. Unquestionably, they sometimes irritated him, and then he abused them, but it is only necessary to read his annotations of his copy of Swedenborg's *Wisdom of the Angels* (now in the British Museum) to realise in the first place that he sometimes misunderstood Swedenborg's position, and secondly, that when he did understand it, he was thoroughly in agreement with it, and that he and the Swedish seer had much in common. Coleridge admired Swedenborg, he gave a good deal of time to studying him (see Coleridge's letter to C. A. Tulk, July 17, 1820), and he, with Boehme, were two of the four " Great Men " unjustly branded, about whom he often thought of writing a " Vindication " (Coleridge's Notes on Noble's Appeal, *Collected Works*, ed. Shedd, 1853 and 1884, vol, v. p. 526).

Emerson owes much to Swedenborg,[1] and Emerson's thought had much influence in England. Carlyle also was attracted to him (see his letter from Chelsea, November 13, 1852) ; Mrs Browning studied him with enthusiasm and spent the winter of 1852-3 in meditation on his philosophy (*Letters*, vol. ii. p. 141), which bore fruit four years later in *Aurora Leigh*.

Coventry Patmore is, however, the English writer most saturated with Swedenborg's thought, and his *Angel in the House* embodies the main features of Swedenborg's peculiar views expressed in *Conjugial Love*, on sex and marriage and their significance. It is not too much to say that Swedenborg influenced and coloured the whole trend of Patmore's thought, and that he was to

[1] See his essay on him in *Representative Men.*

him what Boehme was to Law, the match which
set alight his mystical flame. He says Swedenborg's *Heaven and Hell* " abounds with perception
of the truth to a degree unparalleled perhaps in
uninspired writing," and he asserts that he never
tires of reading him, " he is unfathomably profound and yet simple." [1]

Whatever may be the source or reason, it is
clear that at the end of the eighteenth century
we begin to find a mystical tinge of thought in
several thinkers and writers, such as Burke, Coleridge,
and Thomas Erskine of Linlathen. This increases
in the early nineteenth century, strengthened by
the influence, direct and indirect, of Boehme,
Swedenborg, and the German transcendental philosophers, and this mystical spirit is very marked in
Carlyle, and, as we shall see, in most of the greatest
nineteenth-century poets.

In addition to those writers which are here dealt
with in detail, there is much of the mystic spirit
in others of the same period, to name a few only,
George Meredith, " Fiona Macleod," Christina
Rossetti, and Mrs Browning ; while to-day writers
like " A. E.," W. B. Yeats, and Evelyn Underhill
are carrying on the mystic tradition.

[1] *Memoirs and Correspondence of C. Patmore*, by B. Champneys,
1901, vol. ii. pp. 84, 85.

CHAPTER II

LOVE AND BEAUTY MYSTICS

In studying the mysticism of the English writers, and more especially of the poets, one is at once struck by the diversity of approach leading to unity of end.

"There are," says Plotinus, "different roads by which this end [apprehension of the Infinite] may be reached. The love of beauty, which exalts the poet; that devotion to the One and that ascent of science which makes the ambition of the philosopher; and that love and those prayers by which some devout and ardent soul tends in its moral purity towards perfection. These are the great highways conducting to that height above the actual and the particular, where we stand in the immediate presence of the Infinite, who shines out as from the deeps of the soul."—*Letter to Flaccus.*

We have grouped together our English writers who are mystical in thought, according to the five main pathways by which they have seen the Vision : Love, Beauty, Nature, Wisdom, or Devotion. Even within these groups, the method of approach, the interpretation or application of the Idea, often differs very greatly. For instance, Shelley and Browning may both be called love-mystics ; that is, they look upon love as the solution of the mystery of life, as the link between God and man.

33

To Shelley this was a glorious intuition, which reached him through his imagination, whereas the life of man as he saw it roused in him little but mad indignation, wild revolt, and passionate protest. To Browning this was knowledge—knowledge borne in upon him just because of human life as he saw it, which to him was a clear proof of the great destiny of the race. He would have agreed with Patmore that " you can see the disc of Divinity quite clearly through the smoked glass of humanity, but no otherwise." He found " harmony in immortal souls, spite of the muddy vesture of decay."

The three great English poets who are also fundamentally mystical in thought are Browning, Wordsworth, and Blake. Their philosophy or mystical belief, one in essence, though so differently expressed, lies at the root, as it is also the flower, of their life-work. In others, as in Shelley, Keats, and Rossetti, although it is the inspiring force of their poetry, it is not a flame, burning steadily and evenly, but rather a light flashing out intermittently into brilliant and dazzling radiance. Hence the man himself is not so permeated by it ; and hence results the unsatisfied desire, the almost painful yearning, the recurring disappointment and disillusionment, which we do not find in Browning, Wordsworth, and Blake.

In our first group we have four poets of markedly
different temperaments—Shelley intensely spiritual ;
Rossetti with a strong tinge of sensuousness, of
" earthiness " in his nature ; Browning, the keenly
intellectual man of the world, and Patmore a curious
mixture of materialist and mystic ; yet to all four
love is the secret of life, the one thing worth giving
and possessing.

Shelley believed in a Soul of the Universe, a Spirit
in which all things live and move and have their
being ; which, as one feels in the *Prometheus*, is
unnamable, inconceivable even to man, for " the
deep truth is imageless." His most passionate
desire was not, as was Browning's, for an increased
and ennobled individuality, but for the mystical
fusion of his own personality with this Spirit, this
object of his worship and adoration. To Shelley,
death itself was but the rending of a veil which would
admit us to the full vision of the ideal, which alone
is true life. The sense of unity in all things is most
strongly felt in *Adonais*, where Shelley's maturest
thought and philosophy are to be found ; and
indeed the mystical fervour in this poem, especially
towards the end, is greater than anywhere else
in his writings. The *Hymn to Intellectual Beauty*
is in some ways Shelley's clearest and most obvious expression of his devotion to the Spirit of
Ideal Beauty, its reality to him, and his vow of

dedication to its service. But the *Prometheus* is the most deeply mystical of his poems ; indeed, as Mrs Shelley says, " it requires a mind as subtle and penetrating as Shelley's own to understand the mystic meanings scattered throughout the poem."

Shelley, like Blake, regarded the human imagination as a divine creative force ; Prometheus stands for the human imagination, or the genius of the world ; and it is his union with Asia, the divine Idea, the Spirit of Beauty and of Love, from which a new universe is born. It is this union, which consummates the aspirations of humanity, that Shelley celebrates in the marvellous love-song of Prometheus. As befitted a disciple of Godwin, he believed in the divine potentiality of man, convinced that all good is to be found within man's own being, and that his progress depends on his own will.

> It is our will
> That thus enchains us to permitted ill—
> We might be otherwise—we might be all
> We dream of happy, high, majestical.
> Where is the love, beauty, and truth we seek
> But in our mind ?
>
> *Julian and Maddalo.*

In the allegorical introduction to the *Revolt of Islam*, which is an interesting example of Shelley's

mystical mythology, we have an insight into the
poet's view of the good power in the world. It is
not an almighty creator standing outside mankind,
but a power which suffers and rebels and evolves,
and is, in fact, incarnate in humanity, so that it
is unrecognised by men, and indeed confounded
with evil :—

> And the Great Spirit of Good did creep among
> The nations of mankind, and every tongue
> Cursed and blasphemed him as he passed, for none
> Knew good from evil.

There is no doubt that to Shelley the form assumed
by the divine in man was love. Mrs Shelley, in
her note to *Rosalind and Helen*, says that, " in
his eyes it was the essence of our being, and all woe
and pain arose from the war made against it by
selfishness or insensibility, or mistake " ; and Shelley
himself says, " the great secret of morals is love ;
or a going out of our own nature, and an identifica-
tion of ourselves with the beautiful which exists
in thought, action or person, not our own."

Shelley was always searching for love ; and,
although he knew well, through his study of Plato,
the difference between earthly and spiritual love,
that the one is but the lowest step on the ladder
which leads to the other, yet in actual practice he
confounded the two. He knew that he did so ; and
only a month before his death, he summed up in a

sentence the tragedy of his life. He writes to Mr Gisborne about the *Epipsychidion*, saying that he cannot look at it now, for—

" the person whom it celebrates was a cloud instead of a Juno," and continues, " If you are curious, however, to hear what I am and have been, it will tell you something thereof. It is an idealized history of my life and feelings. I think one is always in love with something or other ; the error—and I confess it is not easy for spirits cased in flesh and blood to avoid it—consists in seeking in a mortal image the likeness of what is, perhaps, eternal."

No poet has a more distinct philosophy of life than Browning. Indeed he has as much a right to a place among the philosophers, as Plato has to one among the poets. Browning is a seer, and pre-eminently a mystic ; and it is especially interesting, as in the case of Plato and St Paul, to encounter this latter quality as a dominating characteristic of the mind of so keen and logical a dialectician. We see at once that the main position of Browning's belief is identical with what we have found to be the characteristic of mysticism—unity under diversity at the centre of all existence. The same essence, the one life, expresses itself through every diversity of form.

He dwells on this again and again :—

> God is seen
> In the star, in the stone, in the flesh, in the soul and the clod.

And through all these forms there is growth upwards.

Indeed, it is only upon this supposition that the poet can account for

> many a thrill
> Of kinship, I confess to, with the powers
> Called Nature : animate, inanimate
> In parts or in the whole, there's something there
> Man-like that somehow meets the man in me.
>
> *Prince Hohenstiel-Schwangau.*

The poet sees that in each higher stage we benefit by the garnered experience of the past ; and so man grows and expands and becomes capable of feeling for and with everything that lives. At the same time the higher is not degraded by having worked in and through the lower, for he distinguishes between the continuous persistent life, and the temporary coverings it makes use of on its upward way ;

> From first to last of lodging, I was I,
> And not at all the place that harboured me.

Humanity then, in Browning's view, is not a collection of individuals, separate and often antagonistic, but one whole.

> When I say " you " 'tis the common soul,
> The collective I mean : the race of Man
> That receives life in parts to live in a whole
> And grow here according to God's clear plan.
>
> *Old Pictures in Florence.*

This sense of unity is shown in many ways : for instance, in Browning's protest against the one-sidedness of nineteenth-century scientific thought, the sharp distinction or gulf set up between science and religion. This sharp cleavage, to the mystic, is impossible. He knows, however irreconcilable the two may appear, that they are but different aspects of the same thing. This is one of the ways in which Browning anticipates the most advanced thought of the present day.

In *Paracelsus* he emphasises the fact that the exertion of power in the intelligence, or the acquisition of knowledge, is useless without the inspiration of love, just as love is waste without power. Paracelsus sums up the matter when he says to Aprile—

> I too have sought to KNOW as thou to LOVE
> Excluding love as thou refusedst knowledge. . . .
>   We must never part . . .
> Till thou the lover, know ; and I, the knower,
> Love—until both are saved.

Arising logically out of this belief in unity, there follows, as with all mystics, the belief in the potential divinity of man, which permeates all Browning's thought, and is continually insisted on in such poems as *Rabbi ben Ezra*, *A Death in the Desert*, and *The Ring and the Book*. He takes for granted the fundamental position of the mystic, that the object of life is to know God ; and according to the poet, in knowing love we learn to know God. Hence it follows that love is the meaning of life, and that he who finds it not

> loses what he lived for
> And eternally must lose it.
>
> *Christina.*

> For life with all it yields of joy and woe
> And hope and fear . . .
> Is just our chance o' the prize of learning love.
>
> *A Death in the Desert.*

This is Browning's central teaching, the key-note of his work and philosophy. The importance of love in life is to Browning supreme, because he holds it to be the meeting-point between God and man. Love is the sublimest conception possible to man ; and a life inspired by it is the highest conceivable form of goodness.

In this exaltation of love, as in several other points, Browning much resembles the German mystic, Meister Eckhart. To compare the two writers in detail would be an interesting task ; it is only possible here to suggest points of resemblance. The following passage from Eckhart suggests several directions in which Browning's thought is peculiarly mystical :—

Intelligence is the youngest faculty in man. . . . The soul in itself is a simple work ; what God works in the simple light of the soul is more beautiful and more delightful than all the other works which He works in all creatures. But foolish people take evil for good and good for evil. But to him who rightly understands, the one work which God works in the soul is better and nobler and higher than all the world. Through that light comes grace. Grace never comes in the intelligence or in the will. If it could come in the intelligence or in the will, the intelligence and the will would have to transcend themselves. On this a master says: There is something secret about it ; and thereby he means the spark of the soul, which alone can apprehend God. The true union between God and the soul takes place in the little spark, which is called the spirit of the soul.[1]

The essential unity of God and man is expressed more than once by Browning in Eckhart's image : as when he speaks of God as Him

> Who never is dishonoured in the spark
> He gave us from his fire of fires.

He is at one with Eckhart, and with all mystics, in his appeal from the intellect to that which is beyond intellect ; in his assertion of the supremacy of feeling, intuition, over knowledge. Browning never wearies of dwelling on the relativity of physical knowledge, and its inadequacy to satisfy man. This is perhaps best brought out in one of the last things he wrote, the " Reverie " in *Asolando* ; but it is dwelt on in nearly all his later and more reflective poems. His maxim was—

> Wholly distrust thy knowledge, then, and trust
> As wholly love allied to ignorance !
> There lies thy truth and safety. . . .
>   Consider well !
> Were knowledge all thy faculty, then God
> Must be ignored : love gains him by first leap.
>   *A Pillar at Sebzevar.*

---

[1] *Selections from the German Mystics*, ed. Inge (Methuen, 1904), p. 4.

Another point of resemblance with Eckhart is suggested by his words : " That foolish people take evil for good, and good for evil." Browning's theory of evil is part of the working-out of his principle of what may be called the coincidence of extreme opposites. This is, of course, part of his main belief in unity, but it is an interesting development of it. This theory is marked all through his writings ; and, although philosophers have dealt with it, he is perhaps the one poet who faces the problem, and expresses himself on the point with entire conviction. His view is that good and evil are purely relative terms (see *The Bean-stripe*), and that one cannot exist without the other. It is evil which alone makes possible some of the divinest qualities in man—compassion, pity, forgiveness, patience. We have seen that Shelley shares this view, " for none knew good from evil " ; and Blake expresses himself very strongly about it, and complains that Plato " knew nothing but the virtues and vices, the good and evil. . . . There is nothing in all that. . . . Everything is good in God's eyes." Mysticism is always a reconcilement of opposites ; and this, as we have seen in connection with science and religion, knowledge and love, is a dominant note of Browning's philosophy. He brings it out most startlingly perhaps in *The Statue and the Bust*, where he shows that in his very

capacity for vice, a man proves his capacity for
virtue, and that a failure of energy in the one implies
a corresponding failure of energy in the other.

At the same time, clear knowledge that evil is
illusion would defeat its own end and paralyse
all moral effort, for evil only exists for the development of good in us.

> Type needs antitype :
> As night needs day, as shine needs shade, so good
> Needs evil : how were pity understood
> Unless by pain ?

This is one reason why Browning never shrank
from the evil in the world, why indeed he expended
so much of his mind and art on the analysis and
dissection of every kind of evil, laying bare for us
the working of the mind of the criminal, the hypocrite, the weakling, and the cynic ; because he held
that—

> Only by looking low, ere looking high
> Comes penetration of the mystery.

There are other ways in which Browning's thought
is especially mystical, as, for instance, his belief
in pre-existence, and his theory of knowledge, for
he, like Plato, believes in the light within the soul,
and holds that—

> To know
> Rather consists in opening out a way
> Whence the imprisoned splendour may escape,

> Than in effecting entry for a light
> Supposed to be without.
>
> *Paracelsus*, Act I.

But the one thought which is ever constant with him, and is peculiarly helpful to the practical man, is his recognition of the value of limitation in all our energies, and the stress he lays on the fact that only by virtue of this limitation can we grow. We should be paralysed else. It is Goethe's doctrine of *Entbehrung*, and it is vividly portrayed in the epistle of Karshish. Paracelsus learns it, and makes it clear to Festus at the end.

The natural result of Browning's theory of evil, and his sense of the value of limitation, is that he should welcome for man the experience of doubt, difficulty, temptation, pain ; and this we find is the case.

> Life is probation and the earth no goal
> But starting point of man . . .
> To try man's foot, if it will creep or climb
> 'Mid obstacles in seeming, points that prove
> Advantage for who vaults from low to high
> And makes the stumbling-block a stepping-stone.

The Ring and the Book: The Pope, 1436-7, 410-13.

It is this trust in unending progress, based on the consciousness of present failure, which is peculiarly inspiriting in Browning's thought, and it is essentially mystical. Instead of shrinking from pain, the mystic prays for it, for, properly met, it means growth.

> Was the trial sore ?
> Temptation sharp ?   Thank God a second time !
> Why comes temptation but for man to meet
> And master and make crouch beneath his foot,
> And so be pedestaled in triumph ?
>> *The Ring and the Book*: The Pope, 1182-92.

Rossetti's mysticism is perhaps a more salient feature in his art than is the case with Browning, and the lines of it, and its place in his work, have been well described by Mr Theodore Watts-Dutton.[1] We can only here indicate wherein it lies, and how it differs from and falls short of the mysticism of Shelley and Browning.   Rossetti, unlike Browning, is not the least metaphysical ; he is not devoured by philosophical curiosity ; he has no desire to solve the riddle of the universe.   All his life he was dominated and fascinated by beauty, one form of which in especial so appealed to him as at times almost to overpower him—the beauty of the face of woman.[2]   But this beauty is not an end in itself ; it is not the desire of possession that so stirs him, but rather an absolute thirst for the knowledge of the mystery which he feels is hiding beneath

[1] See his article on Rossetti in the *Nineteenth Century* for March 1883.

[2] *House of Life*, Sonnet xvii.

and beyond it. Here lies his mysticism. It is
this haunting passion which is the greatest thing
in Rossetti, which inspires all that is best in him
as artist, the belief that beauty is but the expression
or symbol of something far greater and higher,
and that it has kinship with immortal things. For
beauty, which, as Plato has told us, is of all the
divine ideas at once most manifest and most lovable
to man, is for Rossetti the actual and visible symbol
of love, which is at once the mystery and solution
of the secret of life.[1] Rossetti's mystical passion
is perhaps most perfectly expressed in his little
early prose romance, *Hand and Soul*. It is purer
and more austere than much of his poetry, and
breathes an amazing force of spiritual vision. One
wonders, after reading it, that the writer himself
did not attain to a loftier and more spiritual development of life and art ; and one cannot help feeling
the reason was that he did not sufficiently heed
the warning of Plotinus, not to let ourselves become
entangled in sensuous beauty, which will engulf us
as in a swamp.

Coventry Patmore was so entirely a mystic that
it seems to be the first and the last and the only
thing to say about him. His central conviction
is the unity of all things, and hence their mutual
interpretation and symbolic force. There is only

[1] *House of Life*, Sonnets i., xxvii., lxxvii.

one kind of knowledge which counts with him, and that is direct apprehension or perception, the knowledge a man has of Love, by being in love, not by reading about its symptoms. The " touch " of God is not a figure of speech.

"Touch," says Aquinas, "applies to spiritual things as well as to material things. . . . The fulness of intelligence is the obliteration of intelligence. God is then our honey, and we, as St Augustine says, are His ; and who wants to understand honey or requires the *rationale* of a kiss ? " (*Rod, Root, and Flower,* xx.)

Once given the essential idea, to be grasped by the intuitive faculty alone, the world is full of analogies, of natural revelations which help to support and illustrate great truths. Patmore was, however, caught and enthralled by one aspect of unity, by one great analogy, almost to the exclusion of all others. This is that in human love, but above all in wedded love, we have a symbol (that is an expression of a similar force in different material) of the love between God and the soul. What Patmore meant was that in the relationship and attitude of wedded lovers we hold the key to the mystery at the heart of life, and that we have in it a " real apprehension " (which is quite different from real comprehension [1]) of the relationship and attitude of humanity to God. His first wife's love revealed

[1] See *Religio Poetæ*, p. 1.

to him this, which is the basic fact of all his thought and work.

The relationship of the soul to Christ *as His betrothed wife* is the key to the feeling with which prayer and love and honour should be offered to Him. . . . *She* showed me what that relationship involves of heavenly submission and spotless passionate loyalty.[1]

He believed that sex is a relationship at the base of all things natural and divine ;

> Nature, with endless being rife,
>   Parts each thing into " him " and " her "
> And, in the arithmetic of life,
>   The smallest unit is a pair.[2]

This division into two and reconciliation into one, this clash of forces resulting in life, is, as Patmore points out in words curiously reminiscent of those of Boehme, at the root of all existence. All real apprehension of God, he says, is dependent upon the realisation of his triple Personality in one Being.

Nature goes on giving echoes of the same living triplicity in animal, plant, and mineral, every stone and material atom owing its being to the synthesis or " embrace " of the two opposed forces of expansion and contraction. Nothing whatever exists in a single entity but in virtue of its being thesis, antithesis, and synthesis and in humanity and natural life this takes the form of sex, the masculine, the feminine, and the neuter, or third, forgotten sex

[1] *Memoirs*, ed. Champneys, i. 146.
[2] *The Angel in the House.*   Bk. ii. prelude ii.

spoken of by Plato, which is not the absence of the life of sex, but its fulfilment and power, as the electric fire is the fulfilment and power of positive and negative in their " embrace."

The essay from which this passage is taken, *The Bow set in the Cloud*, together with *The Precursor*, give in full detail an exposition of this belief of Patmore's, which was for him "*the burning heart of the Universe.*"

> Female and male God made the man ;
> His image is the whole, not half ;
> And in our love we dimly scan
> The love which is between Himself.[1]

God he conceived of as the great masculine positive force, the soul as the feminine or receptive force, and the meeting of these two, the " mystic rapture " of the marriage of Divinity and Humanity, as the source of all life and joy.

This profound and very difficult theme is treated by Patmore in a manner at once austere and passionate in the exquisite little preludes to the *Angel in the House*, and more especially in the odes, which stand alone in nineteenth-century poetry for poignancy of feeling and depth of spiritual passion. They are the highest expression of " erotic mysticism "[2] in English ; a marvellous combination of flaming ardour and sensuousness of description with purity and austerity of tone. This latter effect

[1] *The Angel in the House*, canto viii. prelude iv.
[2] See pp. 113, 114 below.

is gained largely by the bare and irregular metre, which has a curiously compelling beauty of rhythm and dignity of cadence.

The book into which Patmore put the fullness of his convictions, the *Sponsa Dei*, which he burnt because he feared it revealed too much to a world not ready for it, was, says Mr Gosse, who had read it in manuscript, " a transcendental treatise on Divine desire seen through the veil of human desire." We can guess fairly accurately its tenor and spirit if we read the prose essay *Dieu et ma Dame* and the wonderful ode *Sponsa Dei*, which, happily, the poet did not destroy.

It may be noted that the other human affections and relationships also have for Patmore a deep symbolic value, and two of his finest odes are written, the one in symbolism of mother love, the other in that of father and son.[1]

We learn by human love, so he points out, to realise the possibility of contact between the finite and Infinite, for divinity can only be revealed by voluntarily submitting to limitations. It is " the mystic craving of the great to become the love-captive of the small, while the small has a corresponding thirst for the enthralment of the great." [2]

---

[1] *The Child's Purchase* and *The Toys*, poems, 1 vol., 1906, pp. 287, 354.

[2] *Religio Poetæ*, 1893, p. 163.

And this process of intercourse between God and man is symbolised in the Incarnation, which is not a single event in time, but the culmination of an eternal process. It is the central fact of a man's experience, " for it is going on perceptibly in himself"; and in like manner " the Trinity becomes the only and self-evident explanation of mysteries which are daily wrought in his own complex nature." [1] In this way is it that to Patmore religion is not a question of blameless life or the holding of certain beliefs, but it is " an experimental science " to be lived and to be felt, and the clues to the experiments are to be found in natural human processes and experiences interpreted in the light of the great dogmas of the Christian faith.

For Keats, the avenue to truth and reality took the form of Beauty. The idea, underlying most deeply and consistently the whole of his poetry, is that of the unity of life ; and closely allied with this is the belief in progress, through ever-changing, ever-ascending stages. *Sleep and Poetry, Endymion,* and *Hyperion* represent very well three stages in the poet's thought and art. In *Sleep and Poetry* Keats depicts the growth even in an individual life, and describes the three stages of thought, or attitudes towards life, through which the poet

[1] *Religio Poetæ,* 1893, p. 44.

must pass. They are not quite parallel to the
three stages of the mystical ladder marked out
by Wordsworth in the main body of his poetry,
because they do not go quite so far, but they are
almost exactly analogous to the three stages of mind
he describes in *Tintern Abbey*. The first is mere
animal pleasure and delight in living—

> A pigeon tumbling in clear summer air ;
> A laughing school-boy without grief or care
> Riding the springy branches of an elm.

Then follows simple unreflective enjoyment of
Nature. The next stage is sympathy with human
life, with human grief and joy, which brings a sense
of the mystery of the world, a longing to pierce it
and arrive at its meaning, symbolised in the figure
of the charioteer.

Towards the end of Keats's life this feeling was
growing stronger ; and it is much dwelt upon
in the *Revision of Hyperion*. There he plainly
states that the merely artistic life, the life of the
dreamer, is selfish ; and that the only way to
gain real insight is through contact and sympathy
with human suffering and sorrow ; and in the
lost Woodhouse transcript of the *Revision*, re-
discovered in 1904, there are some lines in which
this point is still further emphasised. The full
realisation of this third stage was not granted to
Keats during his short life ; he had but gleams of it.

The only passage where he describes the ecstasy of vision is in *Endymion* (bk. i., l. 774 ff.), and this resembles in essentials all the other reports of this experience given by mystics. When the mind is ready, anything may lead us to it—music, imagination, love, friendship.

> Feel we these things ?—that moment have we stept
> Into a sort of oneness, and our state
> Is like a floating spirit's.

Keats felt this passage was inspired, and in a letter to Taylor in January 1818 he says, " When I wrote it, it was a regular stepping of the Imagination towards a truth."

In *Endymion*, the underlying idea is the unity of the various elements of the individual soul ; the love of woman is shown to be the same as the love of beauty ; and that in its turn is identical with the love of the principle of beauty in all things. Keats was always very sensitive to the mysterious effects of moonlight, and so for him the moon became a symbol for the great abstract principle of beauty, which, during the whole of his poetic life, he worshipped intellectually and spiritually. " The mighty abstract Idea I have of Beauty in all things stifles the more divided and minute domestic happiness," he writes to his brother George ; and the last two well-known lines of

the *Ode on a Grecian Urn* fairly sum up his
philosophy—

> Beauty is truth, truth Beauty, that is all
> Ye know on earth, and all ye need to know.

So that the moon represents to Keats the eternal
idea, the one essence in all. This is how he writes
of it, in what is an entirely mystical passage in
Endymion—

> . . . As I grew in years, still didst thou blend
> With all my ardours : thou wast the deep glen ;
> Thou wast the mountain-top, the sage's pen,
> The poet's harp, the voice of friends, the sun ;
> Thou wast the river, thou wast glory won ;
> Thou wast my clarion's blast, thou wast my steed,
> My goblet full of wine, my topmost deed :
> Thou wast the charm of women, lovely Moon !

In his fragment of *Hyperion*, Keats shadows
forth the unity of all existence, and gives magnificent
utterance to the belief that change is not decay,
but the law of growth and progress. Oceanus, in
his speech to the overthrown Titans, sums up the
whole meaning as far as it has gone, in verse which
is unsurpassed in English—

> We fall by course of Nature's law, not force
> Of thunder, or of Jove . . .
> . . . on our heels a fresh perfection treads,
> A power more strong in beauty, born of us
> And fated to excel us, as we pass

In glory that old Darkness . . .
. . . for 'tis the eternal law
That first in beauty should be first in might.

This is true mysticism, the mysticism Keats shares with Burke and Carlyle, the passionate belief in continuity of essence through ever-changing forms.

CHAPTER III

VAUGHAN and Wordsworth stand pre-eminent among
our English poets in being almost exclusively oc-
cupied with one theme, the mystical interpretation
of nature.   Both poets are of a meditative, brooding
cast of mind ; but whereas Wordsworth arrives
at his philosophy entirely through personal experience and sensation, Vaughan is more of a mystical
philosopher, deeply read in Plato and the mediæval
alchemists. The constant comparison of natural
with spiritual processes is, on the whole, the most
marked feature of Vaughan's poetry. If man will
but attend, he seems to say to us, everything will
discourse to him of the spirit. He broods on the
silk-worm's change into the butterfly (*Resurrection
and Immortality*) ; he ponders over the mystery
of the continuity of life as seen in the plant, dying
down and entirely disappearing in winter, and
shooting up anew in the spring (*The Hidden Flower*) ;
or, while wandering by his beloved river Usk, he
meditates near the deep pool of a waterfall on its
mystical significance as it seems to linger beneath
the banks and then to shoot onward in swifter

57

course, and he sees in it an image of life beyond the grave. The seed growing secretly in the earth suggests to him the growth of the soul in the darkness of physical matter ; and in *Affliction* he points out that all nature is governed by a law of periodicity and contrast, night and day, sunshine and shower ; and as the beauty of colour can only exist by contrast, so are pain, sickness, and trouble needful for the development of man. These poems are sufficient to illustrate the temper of Vaughan's mind, his keen, reverent observation of nature in all her moods, and his intense interest in the minutest happenings, because they are all manifestations of the one mighty law.

Vaughan appears to have had a more definite belief in pre-existence than Wordsworth, for he refers to it more than once ; and *The Retreate*, which is probably the best known of all his poems and must have furnished some suggestion for the *Immortality Ode*, is based upon it. Vaughan has occasionally an almost perfect felicity of mystical expression, a power he shares with Donne, Keats, Rossetti, and Wordsworth. His ideas then produce their effect through the medium of art, directly on the feelings. The poem called *Quickness* is perhaps the best example of this peculiar quality, which cannot be analysed but must simply be felt ;

or *The World*, with its magnificent symbol in the
opening lines :—

> I saw Eternity the other night,
> Like a great *Ring* of pure and endless light,
>   All calm, as it was bright ;
> And round beneath it, Time, in hours, days, years,
>   Driv'n by the spheres,
> Like a vast shadow mov'd.[1]

Mysticism is the most salient feature of Wordsworth's poetry, for he was one who saw, whose
inward eye was focussed to visions scarce dreamt
of by men. It is because of the strangeness and
unfamiliarity of his vision that he is a difficult
poet to understand, and the key to the understanding
of him is a mystic one. People talk of the difficulty
of Browning, but he is easy reading compared
with a great deal of Wordsworth. It is just the
apparent simplicity of Wordsworth's thought which
is so misleading. A statement about him of the
following kind would be fairly generally accepted as
the truth. Wordsworth was a simple-minded poet
with a passion for nature, he found great joy and
consolation in the contemplation of the beauty of
hills and dales and clouds and flowers, and urged

---

[1] The " Ring " of Eternity is a familiar mystical symbol which
Vaughan doubtless knew in other writers ; for instance as used
by Suso or Ruysbroeck. See *Mysticism*, by E. Underhill, p. 489
and note.

others to find this too ; he lived, and recommended others to live a quiet retired unexciting kind of life, and he preached a doctrine of simplicity and austerity. Now, except that Wordsworth had a passion for Nature, there is not a single true statement here. Wordsworth was not only a poet, he was also a seer, a mystic and a practical psychologist, with an amazingly subtle mind, and an unusual capacity for feeling ; he lived a life of excitement and passion, and he preached a doctrine of magnificence and glory. It was not the beauty of Nature which brought him joy and peace, but the *life* in Nature. He himself had caught a vision of that life, he knew it and felt it, and it transformed the whole of existence for him. He believed that every man could attain this vision which he so fully possessed, and his whole life's work took the form of a minute and careful analysis of the processes of feeling in his own nature, which he left as a guide for those who would tread the same path. It would be correct to say that the whole of his poetry is a series of notes and investigations devoted to the practical and detailed explanation of how he considered this state of vision might be reached. He disdained · no experience—however trivial, apparently—the working of the mind of a peasant child or an idiot boy, the effect produced on his own emotions by a flower, a glowworm, a bird's note, a girl's song; he passed by nothing which might help to throw light on this problem. The experience which Wordsworth was so anxious others should share was the following. He found that when his mind was freed from pre-occupation with disturbing objects, petty cares, "little enmities and low desires," that he could then reach a condition of equilibrium, which he describes as a "wise passiveness," or a "happy stillness of the mind." He believed this condition could be deliberately induced by a kind of relaxation of the will, and by a stilling of the busy intellect and striving desires. It is a purifying process, an emptying out of all that is worrying, self-assertive, and self-seeking. If we can habitually train ourselves and attune our minds to this condition, we may at any moment come across something which will arouse our emotions, and it is then, when our emotions—thus purified— are excited to the point of passion, that our vision becomes sufficiently clear to enable us to gain actual experience of the "central peace subsisting for ever at the heart of endless agitation." Once seen, this vision changes for us the whole of life; it reveals unity in what to our every-day sight appears to be diversity, harmony where ordinarily we hear but discord, and joy, overmastering joy, instead of sorrow.

It is a kind of illumination, whereby in a lightning flash we see that the world is quite different from what it ordinarily appears to be, and when it is over—for the experience is but momentary—it is impossible to describe the vision in precise terms, but the effect of it is such as to inspire and guide the whole subsequent life of the seer. Wordsworth several times depicts this " bliss ineffable " when " all his thought were steeped in feeling." The well-known passage in *Tintern Abbey* already quoted (p. 7) is one of the finest analysis of it left us by any of the seers, and it closely resembles the accounts given by Plotinus and Boehme of similar experiences.

To Wordsworth this vision came through Nature, and for this reason. He believed that all we see round us is alive, beating with the same life which pulsates in us. It is, he says,—

> my faith that every flower
> Enjoys the air it breathes,

and that if we will but listen and look, we will hear and see and feel this central life. This is the pith of the message we find repeated again and again in various forms throughout Wordsworth's poetry, and perhaps best summed up at the end of the fourth book of the *Excursion*, a book which should be closely studied by any one who would explore the secret of the poet's outlook upon life. He tells us in the *Prelude* (Book iii.) that even in boyhood it was by this feeling he " mounted to community with highest truth "—

> To every natural form, rock, fruits, or flower,
> Even the loose stones that cover the highway,
> I gave a moral life : I saw them feel,
> Or linked them to some feeling : the great mass
> Lay bedded in a quickening soul, and all
> That I beheld respired with inward meaning.

Wordsworth, in short, was haunted by the belief that the secret of the universe is written clearly all round us, could we but train and purify our mind and emotions so as to behold it. He believed that we are in something the same attitude towards Nature as an illiterate untrained person might be in the presence of a book containing the philosophy of Hegel. To the educated trained thinker, who by long and arduous discipline has developed his mental powers, that book contains the revelation of the thought of a great mind ; whereas to the uneducated person it is merely a bundle of paper with words printed on it. He can handle it, touch it, see it, he can read the words, he can even understand many of them separately, but the essence of the book and its meaning remains closed to him until he can effect some alteration in himself which will enable him to understand it.

Wordsworth's claim is that he had discovered by his own experience a way to effect the necessary alteration in ourselves which will enable us to catch glimpses of the truths expressing themselves all round us. It is a great claim, but he would seem to have justified it.

It is interesting that the steps in the ladder of perfection, as described by Wordsworth, are precisely analogous to the threefold path or " way " of the religious and philosophic mystic, an ethical system or rule of life, of which, very probably, Wordsworth had never heard.

The mystic vision was not attained by him, any more than by others, without deliberate renunciation. He lays great stress upon this ; and yet it is a point in his teaching sometimes overlooked. He insists repeatedly upon the fact that before any one can taste of these joys of the spirit, he must be purified, disciplined, self-controlled. He leaves us a full account of his purgative stage. Although he started life with a naturally pure and austere temperament, yet he had deliberately to crush out certain strong passions to which he was liable, as well as all personal ambition, all love of power, all desire for fame or money ; and to confine himself to the contemplation of such objects as—

excite
No morbid passions, no disquietude,
No vengeance and no hatred.

In the *Recluse* he records how he deliberately fought,
and bent to other uses, a certain wild passionate
delight he felt in danger, a struggle or victory over
a foe, in short, some of the primitive instincts of
a strong, healthy animal, feelings which few would
regard as reprehensible. These natural instincts,
this force and energy, good in themselves, Wordsworth did not crush, but deliberately turned into a
higher channel.

At the end of the *Prelude* he makes his confession
of the sins he did not commit.

> Never did I, in quest of right and wrong,
> Tamper with conscience from a private aim ;
> Nor was in any public hope the dupe
> Of selfish passions ; nor did ever yield
> Wilfully to mean cares or low pursuits.

Such a confession, or rather boast, in the mouth of
almost any other man would sound hypocritical or
self-complacent ; but with Wordsworth, we feel it
is the bare truth told us for our help and guidance,
as being the necessary and preliminary step. It
is a high standard which is held up before us, even
in this first stage, for it includes, not merely the
avoidance of all obvious sins against man and
society, but a tuning-up, a transmuting of the whole
nature to high and noble endeavour. Wordsworth
found his reward, in a settled state of calm serenity,
" consummate happiness," " wide-spreading, steady,

calm, contemplative," and, as he tells us in the
fourth book of the *Prelude*, on one evening during
that summer vacation,

> Gently did my soul
> Put off her veil, and, self-transmuted, stood
> Naked, as in the presence of her God.

When the mind and soul have been prepared,
the next step is concentration, aspiration. Then
it is borne in upon the poet that in the infinite and
in the eternal alone can we find rest, can we find
ourselves ; and towards this infinitude we must
strive with unflagging ardour ;

> Our destiny, our being's heart and home,
> Is with infinitude, and only there.
>
> *Prelude*, Book vi. 604.

The result of this aspiration towards the infinite
is a quickening of consciousness, upon which follows
the attainment of the third or unitive stage, the
moment when man can " breathe in worlds to which
the heaven of heavens is but a veil," and perceive
" the forms whose kingdom is where time and place
are not." Such minds—

> need not extraordinary calls
> To rouse them ; in a world of life they live,
> By sensible impressions not enthralled,
>   . . . the highest bliss
> That flesh can know is theirs—the consciousness
> Of Whom they are.
>
> *Prelude,* Book xiv. 105, 113,

Wordsworth possessed in a peculiar degree a mystic sense of infinity, of the boundless, of the opening-out of the world of our normal finite experience into the transcendental ; and he had a rare power of putting this into words. It was a feeling which, as he tells us in the *Prelude* (Book xiii.), he had from earliest childhood, when the disappearing line of the public highway—

> Was like an invitation into space
> Boundless, or guide into eternity,

a feeling which, applied to man, gives that inspiriting certitude of boundless growth, when the soul has—

> . . . an obscure sense
> Of possible sublimity, whereto
> With growing faculties she doth aspire.

It is at this point, and on this subject, that Wordsworth's poetical and ethical imagination are most nearly fused. This fusion is far from constant with him ; and the result is that there are tracts of his writings where the sentiments are excellent, the philosophy illuminating, but the poetry is not great : it does not awaken the " transcendental feeling." [1] The moments when this condition is most fully attained by Wordsworth occur when, by sheer force of poetic imagination combined with

[1] See the illuminating description of this essentially mystic feeling given by J. Stewart in *The Myths of Plato*, Introduction, pp. 39 *et seq*

spiritual insight, in some mysterious and indescribable way, he flashes upon us a sensation of boundless infinity. Herein consists the peculiar magic of such a poem as *Stepping Westward* ; and there is a touch of the same feeling in the *Solitary Reaper*.

It is hardly necessary to dwell on other mystical elements in Wordsworth, such as his belief in the one law governing all things, "from creeping plant to sovereign man," and the hint of belief in pre-existence in the *Ode on Immortality*. His attitude towards life as a whole is to be found in a few lines in the " after-thought " to the Duddon sonnets.

> The Form remains, the Function never dies ;
> While we, the brave, the mighty and the wise,
> We Men, who in our morn of youth defied
> The elements, must vanish :—be it so !
> Enough, if something from our hands have power
> To live, and act, and serve the future hour ;
> And if, as toward the silent tomb we go,
> Through love, through hope, and faith's transcendent dower,
> We feel that we are greater than we know.

Richard Jefferies is closely akin to Wordsworth in his overpowering consciousness of the life in nature. This consciousness is the strongest force in him, so that at times he is almost submerged by it, and he loses the sense of outward things. In this condition of trance the sense of time vanishes, there is, he asserts, no such thing, no past or future, only now, which is eternity. In *The Story of my Heart*, a rhapsody of mystic experience and aspiration, he describes in detail several such moments of exaltation or trance. He seems to be peculiarly sensitive to sunshine. As the moon typifies to Keats the eternal essence in all things, so to Jefferies the sun seems to be the physical expression or symbol of the central Force of the world, and it is through gazing on sunlight that he most often enters into the trance state.

Standing, one summer's morning, in a recess on London Bridge, he looks out on the sunshine " burning on steadfast," " lighting the great heaven ; gleaming on my finger-nail."

" I was intensely conscious of it," he writes, " I felt it ; I felt the presence of the immense powers of the universe ; I felt out into the depths of the ether. So intensely conscious of the sun, the sky, the limitless space, I felt too in the midst of eternity then, in the midst of the supernatural, among the immortal, and the greatness of the material realised the spirit. By these I saw my soul ; by these I knew the supernatural to be more intensely real than the sun. I touched the supernatural, the immortal, there that moment."[1]

When he reaches this state, outer things drop away,[2] and he seems to become lost, and absorbed into the being of the universe. He partakes, momentarily, of a larger, fuller life, he drinks in vitality through nature. The least blade of grass, he says, or the greatest oak, " seemed like exterior

[1] *The Story of my Heart*, pp. 87, 88.   [2] *Ibid.*, p. 76.

nerves and veins for the conveyance of feeling to me. Sometimes a very ecstasy of exquisite enjoyment of the entire visible universe filled me." [1]

This great central Life Force, which Jefferies, like Wordsworth, seemed at moments to touch, he, in marked contrast to other mystics, refuses to call God. For, he says, what we understand by deity is the purest form of mind, and he sees no mind in nature. It is a force without a mind, " more subtle than electricity, but absolutely devoid of consciousness, and with no more feeling than the force which lifts the tides." [2] Yet this cannot content him, for later he declares there must be an existence higher than deity, towards which he aspires and presses with the whole force of his being. " Give me," he cries, " to live the deepest soul-life now and always with this ' Highest Soul.' " [3]

This thrilling consciousness of spiritual life felt through nature, coupled with passionate aspiration to be absorbed in that larger life, are the two main features of the mysticism of Richard Jefferies.

His books, and especially *The Story of my Heart*, contain, together with the most exquisite nature description, a rich and vivid record of sensation, feeling, and aspiration. But it is a feeling which, though vivifying, can only be expressed in general terms, and it carries with it no vision and no philo-

[1] *The Story of my Heart*, p. 199.   [2] *Ibid.*, p. 71.   [3] *Ibid.*; p. 74.

sophy. It is almost entirely emotional, and it is as
an emotional record that it is of value, for Jefferies'
intellectual reflections are, for the most part, curiously contradictory and unconvincing.

The certainty and rapture of this experience of
spiritual emotion is all the more amazing when we
remember that the record of it was written in agony,
when he was wrecked with mortal illness and his
nerves were shattered with pain. For with him,
as later with Francis Thompson, physical pain and
material trouble seemed to serve only to direct him
towards and to enhance the glory of the spiritual
vision.

CHAPTER IV

PHILOSOPHICAL MYSTICS

THE mystical sense may be called philosophical in all those writers who present their convictions in a philosophic form calculated to appeal to the intellect as well as to the emotions. These writers, as a rule, though not always, are themselves markedly intellectual, and their primary concern therefore is with truth or wisdom. Thus Donne, William Law, Burke, Coleridge, and Carlyle are all predominantly intellectual, while Traherne, Emily Brontë, and Tennyson clothe their thoughts to some extent in the language of philosophy.

The dominating characteristic of Donne is intellectuality ; and this may partly account for the lack in him of some essentially mystical qualities, more especially reverence, and that ascension of thought so characteristic of Plato and Browning. These shortcomings are very well illustrated in that extraordinary poem, *The Progress of the Soul*. The idea is a mystical one, derived from Pythagorean philosophy, and has great possibilities, which Donne entirely fails to utilise ; for, instead of following the soul upwards on its way, he depicts it as merely

jumping about from body to body, and we are
conscious of an entire lack of any lift or grandeur
of thought. This poem helps us to understand
how it was that Donne, though so richly endowed
with intellectual gifts, yet failed to reach the highest
rank as a poet. He was brilliant in particulars,
but lacked the epic qualities of breadth, unity, and
proportion, characteristics destined to be the dis-
tinctive marks of the school of which he is looked
upon as the founder.

Apart from this somewhat important defect,
Donne's attitude of mind is essentially mystical.
This is especially marked in his feeling about the
body and natural law, in his treatment of love,
and in his conception of woman. The mystic's
postulate—if we could know ourselves, we should
know all—is often on Donne's lips, as for instance
in that curious poem written in memory of Elizabeth
Drury, on the second anniversary of her death. It
is perhaps best expressed in the following verse :

> But we know our selves least ; Mere outward shews
>   Our mindes so store,
> That our soules, no more than our eyes disclose
> But forme and colour. Onely he who knowes
>   Himselfe, knowes more.
>
> *Ode : Of our Sense of Sinne.*

One of the marked characteristics of Donne's poetry
is his continual comparison of mental and spiritual

with physical processes. This sense of analogy prevailing throughout nature is with him very strong. The mystery of continual flux and change particularly attracts him, as it did the Buddhists[1] and the early Greek thinkers, and Nettleship's remarks about the nature of bread and unselfishness are akin to the following comparison :—

> Dost thou love
> Beauty ? (And beauty worthy'st is to move)
> Poor cousened cousener, *that* she, and *that* thou,
> Which did begin to love, are neither now ;
> Next day repaires (but ill) last dayes decay.
> Nor are, (although the river keepe the name)
> Yesterdaies waters, and to-daies the same.
> > *Of the Progresse of the Soule.   The second
> > Anniversarie,* 389-96.

Donne believes firmly in man's potential greatness, and the power within his own soul :

> Seeke wee then our selves in our selves ; for as
> Men force the Sunne with much more force to passe,
> By gathering his beames with a chrystall glasse ;
>
> So wee, If wee into our selves will turne,
> Blowing our sparkes of virtue, may out-burne
> The straw, which doth about our hearts sojourne.
> > *Letter to Mr Rowland Woodward.*

And although, in the *Progress of the Soul*, he failed

---

[1] See *Compendium of Philosophy*, a mediæval digest of the Abhidhamma, translated by S. Z. Aung and Mrs Rhys Davids, 1910, 152 f.

to give expression to it, yet his belief in progress is unquenchable. He fully shares the mystic's view that " man, to get towards Him that's Infinite, must first be great " (*Letter to the Countess of Salisbury*).

In his treatment of love, Donne's mystical attitude is most clearly seen. He holds the Platonic conception, that love concerns the soul only, and is independent of the body, or bodily presence ; and he is the poet, who, at his best, expresses this idea in the most dignified and refined way. The reader feels not only that Donne believes it, but that he has in some measure experienced it ; whereas with his imitators it degenerated into little more than a fashionable " conceit." The *Undertaking* expresses the discovery he has made of this higher and deeper kind of love ; and in the *Ecstasy* he describes the union of the souls of two lovers in language which proves his familiarity with the description of ecstasy given by Plotinus (*Enn.* vi. 9, § 11). The great value of this spiritual love is that it is unaffected by time and space, a belief which is nowhere more exquisitely expressed than in the refrain of his little song, *Soul's Joy*.[1]

[1] We cannot agree with Prof. Grierson, who, in his fine recent edition of the poet (*Donne's Poems*, Oxford, 1912, vol. ii., pp. cxxxv.-vi.), holds that the style and tone of this song point to Donne not being the author. For these very qualities it would seem indubitably to be his.

> O give no way to griefe,
> But let beliefe
>   Of mutuall love,
> This wonder to the vulgar prove
>   Our Bodyes, not wee move.

In one of his verse letters to the Countess of Hunting-don[1] he explains how true love cannot be desire :

> 'Tis love, but with such fatall weaknesse made,
> That it destroyes it selfe with its owne shade.

He goes still further in the poem entitled *Negative Love*, where he says that love is such a passion as can only be defined by negatives, for it is above apprehension, and his language here is closely akin to the description of the One or the Good given by Plotinus in the sixth Ennead.

Thomas Traherne is a mystical writer of singular charm and originality.   The manuscripts of his poems and his prose *Meditations*, a kind of spiritual autobiography and notebook, were only discovered and printed quite recently, and they form a valuable addition to the mystical literature of the seventeenth century.

He has affinities with Vaughan, Herbert, and Sir Thomas Browne, with Blake and with Wordsworth. He is deeply sensitive to the beauty of the natural world, and he insists on the necessity for rejoicing in this beauty if we are really to live.   By love

[1] Surely also by Donne, but see Grierson, vol. ii., pp. cxxxviii-ix.

alone is God to be approached and known, he says, but this love must not be finite. " He must be loved in all with an unlimited love, even in all His doings, in all His friends, in all His creatures." In a prose passage of sustained beauty Traherne thus describes the attitude towards earth which is needful before we can enter heaven.

You never enjoy the world aright, till the Sea itself floweth in your veins, till you are clothed with the heavens, and crowned with the stars: . . . Till you can sing and rejoice and delight in God, as misers do in gold, and Kings in sceptres, you never enjoy the world.

Till your spirit filleth the whole world, and the stars are your jewels; . . . till you love men so as to desire their happiness, with a thirst equal to the zeal of your own : till you delight in God for being good to all: you never enjoy the world. . . . The world is a mirror of infinite beauty, yet no man sees it. It is a Temple of Majesty, yet no man regards it. It is a region of Light and Peace, did not men disquiet it. It is the Paradise of God. . . . It is the place of Angels and the Gate of Heaven.[1]

He is for ever reiterating, in company with all the mystics, that

'Tis not the object, but the light
That maketh Heaven : 'tis a purer sight.

He shares Wordsworth's rapture in the life of nature, and Browning's interest in his fellow-men ; he has Shelley's belief in the inner meaning of love, and much of Keats's worship of beauty, and he expresses this in an original and lyrical prose

[1] *Centuries of Meditations,* ed. Dobell, 1908, pp. 20, 21.

of quite peculiar and haunting beauty. He has embodied his main ideas, with a good deal of repetition, both in prose and verse, but it is invariably the prose version, probably written first, which is the most arresting and vigorous.

His *Meditations* well repay careful study ; they are full of wisdom and of an imaginative philosophy, expressed in pithy and telling form, which continually reminds the reader of Blake's *Proverbs of Hell*.

> To have no principles or to live beside them, is equally miserable.
> Philosophers are not those that speak but do great things.
> All men see the same objects, but do not equally understand them.
> Souls to souls are like apples, one being rotten rots another.

This kind of saying abounds on every page. Some of his more sustained philosophic passages are also noteworthy ; such, for instance, is his comparison of the powers of the soul to the rays of the sun, which carry light in them unexpressed until they meet an object (*Meditations*, second century, No. 78). But Traherne's most interesting contribution to the psychology of mysticism is his account of his childhood and the " vision splendid " that he brought with him. Even more to him than to Vaughan or Wordsworth,

> The earth, and every common sight
> . . . did seem
> Apparelled in celestial light,

and his description of his feelings and spiritual

insight are both astonishing and convincing. A number of his poems are devoted to this topic (*The Salutation, Wonder, Eden, Innocence, The Rapture, The Approach,* and others), but it is the prose account which must be given.

All appeared new, and strange at first, inexpressibly rare and delightful and beautiful. I was a little stranger, which at my entrance into the world was saluted and surrounded with innumerable joys. . . . The corn was orient and immortal wheat, which never should be reaped, nor was ever sown. I thought it had stood from everlasting to everlasting. The dust and stones of the street were as precious as gold : the gates were at first the end of the world. The green trees when I saw them first . . . transported and ravished me, their sweetness and unusual beauty made my heart to leap, and almost mad with ecstasy, they were such strange and wonderful things. The Men ! O what venerable and reverend creatures did the aged seem ! Immortal Cherubims ! And young men glittering and sparkling Angels, and maids strange seraphic pieces of life and beauty ! Boys and girls tumbling in the street, and playing, were moving jewels. I knew not that they were born or should die ; but all things abided eternally as they were in their proper places. . . . The city seemed to stand in Eden, or to be built in Heaven.[1]

It is necessary to quote at some length, because it is the way in which Traherne expresses his experiences or reflections which is the moving and original thing about him. This last passage seems to anticipate something of the magic of Keats in the *Ode to a Nightingale* or the *Grecian Urn,* the sense of continuity, and of eternity expressed in time.

[1] *Centuries of Meditations,* pp. 156-58.

Traherne's account of the gradual dimming of this early radiance, and his enforced change of values is equally unusual. Only with great difficulty did his elders persuade him " that the tinselled ware upon a hobby-horse was a fine thing " and that a purse of gold was of any value, but by degrees when he found that all men prized things he did not dream of, and never mentioned those he cared for, then his " thoughts were blotted out ; and at last all the celestial, great and stable treasures, to which I was born, as wholly forgotten, if as they had never been."

But he remembered enough of those early glories to realise that if he would regain happiness, he must " become, as it were, a little child again," get free of " the burden and cumber of devised wants," and recapture the value and the glory of the common things of life.

He was so resolutely bent on this that when he had left college and come into the country and was free, he lived upon £10 a year, fed on bread and water, and, like George Fox, wore a leather suit. Thus released from all worldly cares, he says, through God's blessing, " I live a free and kingly life as if the world were turned again into Eden, or much more, as it is at this day."

In Emily Brontë we have an unusual type of mystic. Indeed she is one of the most strange

and baffling figures in our literature. We know
in truth very little about her, but that little is
quite unlike what we know about any one else.
It is now beginning to be realised that she was
a greater and more original genius than her famous
sister, and that strong as were Charlotte's passion
and imagination, the passion and imagination of
Emily were still stronger. She had, so far as
we can tell, peculiarly little actual experience of
life, her material interests were bounded by her
family, the old servant Tabby, the dogs, and the
moors. For the greater part of her thirty years
of life she did the work of a servant in the little
parsonage house on the edge of the graveyard.
She can have read little of philosophy or metaphysics,
and probably had never heard of the mystics ; she
was brought up in a narrow, crude, and harshly
material creed ; yet her own inner experience,
her touch with the secret of life, enabled her to
write the remarkable series of poems the peculiar
and haunting quality of which has as yet scarcely
been recognised. They are strong and free and
certain, hampered by no dogma, weighted by no
explanation, but containing — in the simplest
language—the record of the experience and the
vision of a soul. Emily Brontë lived remote,
unapproachable, self-sufficing and entirely detached,
yet consumed with a fierce, unquenchable love of

life and of nature, of the life which withheld from
her all the gifts most prized of men, love, friendship,
experience, recognition, fame ; and of the nature
which she knew only on a circumscribed space of
the wild Yorkshire moors.

In her poems her mysticism is seen principally
in two ways : in her unerring apprehension of
values, of the illusory quality of material things,
even of the nature she so loved, together with
the certain vision of the one Reality behind
all forms. This, and her description of ecstasy,
of the all-sufficing joy of the inner life of one
who has tasted this experience, mark her out
as being among those who have seen, and who
know. In *The Prisoner*, the speaker, a woman,
is " confined in triple walls," yet in spite of
bolts and bars and dungeon gloom she holds
within herself an inextinguishable joy and un-
measured freedom brought to her every night by
a " messenger."

> He comes with western winds, with evening's wandering airs,
> With that clear dusk of heaven that brings the thickest stars.
> Winds take a pensive tone, and stars a tender fire,
> And visions rise, and change, that kill me with desire.
>
> .   .   .   .
>
> But, first, a hush of peace—a soundless calm descends ;
> The struggle of distress, and fierce impatience ends ;
> Mute music soothes my breast—unuttered harmony,
> That I could never dream, till Earth was lost to me.

Then dawns the Invisible ; the Unseen its truth reveals ;
My outward sense is gone, my inward essence feels :
Its wings are almost free—its home, its harbour found,
Measuring the gulf, it stoops and dares the final bound.

Oh ! dreadful is the check—intense the agony—
When the ear begins to hear, and the eye begins to see ;
When the pulse begins to throb, the brain to think again ;
The soul to feel the flesh, and the flesh to feel the chain.

This is the description—always unmistakable—of
the supreme mystic experience, the joy of the outward flight, the pain of the return, and it could only
have been written by one who in some measure
had knowledge of it. This, together with the
exquisite little poem *The Visionary*, which describes
a similar experience, and *The Philosopher*, stand
apart as expressions of spiritual vision, and are
among the most perfect mystic poems in English.

Her realisation of the meaning of common things,
her knowledge that they hold the secret of the
universe, and her crystallisation of this in verse,
place her with Blake and Wordsworth.

What have those lonely mountains worth revealing ?
More glory and more grief than I can tell :
The earth that wakes *one* human heart to feeling
Can centre both the worlds of Heaven and Hell.

And finally, the sense of continuous life—one
central, all-sustaining Life—of the oneness of God
and man, has never been more nobly expressed
than in what is her best-known poem, the last lines
she ever wrote :—

O God within my breast,
Almighty, ever-present Deity !
Life—that in me has rest,
As I—undying Life—have power in Thee !

. . . . . .

With wide-embracing love
Thy spirit animates eternal years,
Pervades and broods above,
Changes, sustains, dissolves, creates, and rears.

Though earth and man were gone,
And suns and universes ceased to be,
And Thou wert left alone,
Every existence would exist in Thee.

Tennyson differs widely from the other poets whom we are considering in this connection. He was not born with the mystical temperament, but, on the contrary, he had a long and bitter struggle with his own doubts and questionings before he wrested from them peace. There is nothing of mystic calm or strength in the lines—

Oh, yet we trust that somehow good
Will be the final goal of ill.

He has no mystic rapture in Nature like Wordsworth,

I found Him not in world or sun
Or eagle's wing, or insect's eye ;

no mystic interpretation of life as had Browning, no yearning for union with the spirit of love and beauty as had Shelley. Tennyson's mysticism came, as it were, rather in spite of himself, and is based on one thing only—experience. He states his position quite clearly in *In Memoriam*, cxxiv. As is well known, he had from time to time á certain peculiar experience, which he describes fully both in prose and verse, a touch at intervals throughout his life of " ecstasy," and it was on this he based his deepest belief. He has left several prose accounts of this mental state, which often came to him through repeating his own name silently,

till all at once, as it were, out of the intensity of the conscious-ness of individuality, the individuality itself seemed to resolve and fade away into boundless being, and this not a confused state, but the clearest of the clearest, the surest of the surest, utterly beyond words, where death was an almost laughable impossibility, the loss of personality (if so it were) seeming no extinction, but the only true life.[1]

It is a somewhat similar experience which is described in *In Memoriam*, xcv.

> And all at once it seem'd at last
> The living soul was flash'd on mine,
>
> And mine in this was wound, and whirl'd
> About empyreal heights of thought,
> And came on that which is, and caught
> The deep pulsations of the world.

And again in the conclusion of the *Holy Grail*—

> Let visions of the night or of the day
> Come, as they will ; and many a time they come,

Life of Tennyson, by his son, 1905, p. 268 ; see also pp· 816, 820.

Until this earth he walks on seems not earth,
This light that strikes his eyeball is not light,
This air that strikes his forehead is not air
But vision—yea, his very hand and foot—
In moments when he feels he cannot die,
And knows himself no vision to himself,
Nor the high God a vision, nor that One
Who rose again.

" These three lines," said Tennyson, speaking of
the last three quoted, " are the (spiritually) central
lines in the Idylls." They are also the central
lines in his own philosophy, for it was the experience of this " vision " that inspired all his deepest
convictions with regard to the unity of all things,
the reality of the unseen, and the persistence of
life.

The belief in the impotence of intellectual knowledge is very closely connected, it is indeed based,
upon these " gleams " of ecstasy. The prologue
to *In Memoriam* (written when the poem was com-
pleted) seems to sum up his faith after many years
of struggle and doubt ; but it is in the most philosophical, as well as one of the latest, of his poems,
The Ancient Sage, that we find this attitude most
fully expressed. Tennyson wrote of it : " The
whole poem is very personal. The passages about
' Faith ' and ' the Passion of the Past ' were more
especially my own personal feelings." Through
the mouth of the Sage, the poet declares in impas-

sioned words the position of the mystic, and points out the impotence of sense-knowledge in dealing with that which is beyond either the senses or the reason :

> For Knowledge is the swallow on the lake
> That sees and stirs the surface-shadow there
> But never yet hath dipt into the abysm.

Tennyson, like Wordsworth, emphasises the truth that the only way in which man can gain real knowledge and hear the " Nameless " is by diving or sinking into the centre of his own being. There is a great deal of Eastern philosophy and mysticism in the *Ancient Sage*, as, for instance, the feeling of the unity of all existence to the point of merging the personality into the universal.

> But that one ripple on the boundless deep
> Feels that the deep is boundless, and itself
> For ever changing form, but evermore
> One with the boundless motion of the deep.

We know that Tennyson had been studying the philosophy of Lâo-Tsze about this time ; yet, though this is, as it were, grafted on to the poet's mind, still we may take it as being his genuine and deepest conviction. The nearest approach to a definite statement of it to be found in his poems is in the few stanzas called *The Higher Pantheism*, which he sent to be read at the first meeting of the Metaphysical Society in 1869.

Speak to Him thou for He hears, and Spirit with Spirit can meet—
Closer is He than breathing, and nearer than hands and feet.

. . . .

And the ear of man cannot hear, and the eye of man cannot see;
But if we could see and hear, this Vision—were it not He ?

In William Law, Burke, Coleridge, and Carlyle,
we have a succession of great English prose-writers
whose work and thought is permeated by a mystical philosophy. Of these four, Law is, during
his later life, by far the most consistently and predominantly mystical.

As has been indicated, there were many strains
of influence which in the seventeenth century
tended to foster mystical thought in England.
The group of Cambridge Platonists, to which Henry
More belonged, gave new expression to the great
Neo-platonic ideas, but in addition to this a strong
vein of mysticism had been kept alive in Amsterdam,
where the exiled Separatists had gone in 1593.
They flourished there and waxed strong, and sent
back to England during the next century a continual
stream of opinion and literature. To this source
can be traced the ideas which inspired alike the
Quakers, the Seekers, the Behmenists, the Familists,
and numberless other sects who all embodied a
reaction against forms and ceremonies, which, in
ceasing to be understood, had become lifeless.
These sects were, up to a certain point, mystical

in thought, for they all believed in the " inner light," in the immediate revelation of God within the soul as the all-important experience.

The persecutions of the Quakers under Charles II. tended to withdraw them from active philanthropy, and to throw them more in the direction of a personal and contemplative religion. It was then that the writings of Madame Bourignon, Madame Guyon, and Fénelon became popular, and were much read among a certain section of thinkers, while the influence of the teachings of Jacob Boehme, whose works had been translated into English between the years 1644 and 1692, can be traced, in diverse ways. They impressed themselves on the thought of the founders of the Society of Friends, they produced a distinct " Behmenist " sect, and it would seem that the idea of the three laws of motion first reached Newton through his eager study of Boehme. But all this has nothing directly to do with literature, and would not concern us here were it not that in the eighteenth century William Law came into touch with many of these mystical thinkers, and that he has embodied in some of the finest prose in our language a portion of the " inspired cobbler's " vision of the universe.

Law's character is one of considerable interest. Typically English, and in intellect typically of the eighteenth century, logical, sane, practical, he is not, at first sight, the man one would expect to find in sympathy with the mystics. Sincerity is the keynote of his whole nature, sincerity of thought, of belief, of speech, and of life. Sincerity implies courage, and Law was a brave man, never shirking the logical outcome of his convictions, from the day when he ruined his prospects at Cambridge, to the later years when he suffered his really considerable reputation to be eclipsed by his espousal of an uncomprehended and unpopular mysticism. He had a keen rather than a profound intellect, and his thought is lightened by brilliant flashes of wit or of grim satire. We can tell, however, from his letters and his later writings, that underneath a severe and slightly stiff exterior, were hidden emotion, enthusiasm, and great tenderness of feeling.

By middle life Law was well known as a most able and brilliant writer on most of the burning theological questions of the day, as well as the author of one of the best loved and most widely read practical and ethical treatises in the language, *A Serious Call to a Devout and Holy Life.* These earlier writings are by far the best known of his works, and it is with the *Serious Call* that his name will always be associated.

Until middle age he showed no marked mystical tendency, although we know that from the time he was an undergraduate he was a " diligent reader " of mystical books, and that he had studied, among others, Dionysius the Areopagite, Ruysbroek, Tauler, Suso, and the seventeenth century Quietists, Fénelon, Madame Guyon, and Antoinette Bourignon.

When, however, he was about forty-six (*c.* 1733), he came across the writings of the seer who set his whole nature aglow with spiritual fervour, so that when he first read his works they put him into " a perfect sweat." Jacob Boehme—or Behmen, as he has usually been called in England—(1575-1624), the illiterate and untrained peasant shoemaker of Görlitz, is one of the most amazing phenomena in the history of mysticism, a history which does not lack wonders. His work has so much influenced later mystical thought and philosophy that a little space must be devoted to him here. He lived outwardly the quiet, hard-working life of a simple German peasant, but inwardly—like his fellow-seer Blake—he lived in a glory of illumination, which by flashes revealed to him the mysteries and splendours he tries in broken and faltering words to record. He saw with the eye of his mind into the heart of things, and he wrote down as much of it as he could express.

The older mystics—eastern and western alike—had laid stress on unity as seen in the nature of God and all things. No one more fully believed in ulti-mate unity than did Boehme, but he lays peculiar stress on the duality, or more accurately, the trinity in unity ; and the central point of his philosophy is the fundamental postulate that all manifestation necessitates opposition. He asserted the uniformity of law throughout all existence, physical and spiritual, and this law, which applies all through nature, divine and human alike, is that nothing can reveal itself without resistance, good can only be known through evil, and weakness through strength, just as light is only visible when reflected by a dark body.

Thus when God, the Triune Principle, or *Will* under three aspects, desires to become manifest, He divides the Will into two, the " yes " and the " no," and so founds an eternal contrast to Himself out of His own hidden Nature, in order to enter into struggle with it, and finally to discipline and assimilate it. The object of all manifested nature is the transforming of the will which says " No " into the will which says " Yes," and this is brought about by seven organising spirits or forms. The first three of these bring nature out of the dark element to the point where contact with the light is possible. Boehme calls them harshness, attraction, and anguish, which in modern terms are contraction, expansion, and rotation. The first two are in deadly antagonism, and being forced into collision, form an endless whirl of movement.

These two forces with their resultant effect are to be found all through manifested nature, within man and without, and are called by different names : good, evil and life, God, the devil and the world, homogeneity, heterogeneity, strain, or the three laws of motion, centripetal and centrifugal force, resulting in rotation. They are the outcome of the " nature " or " no " will, and are the basis of all manifestation. They are the " power " of God, apart from the " love," hence their conflict is terrible. When spirit and nature approach and meet, from the shock a new form is liberated, lightning or fire, which is the fourth moment or essence. With the lightning ends the development of the negative triad, and the evolution of the three higher forms then begins ; Boehme calls them light or love, sound and substance ; they are of the spirit, and in them contraction, expansion, and rotation are repeated in a new sense. The first three forms give the stuff or strength of being, the last three manifest the quality of being good or bad, and evolution can proceed in either direction.

The practical and ethical result of this living unity of nature is the side which most attracted Law, and it is one which is as simple to state as it is difficult to apply. Boehme's philosophy is one which can only be apprehended by living it. Will, or desire, is the radical force in man as it is in nature and in the Godhead, and until that is turned towards the light, any purely historical or intellectual knowledge of these things is as useless as if hydrogen were to expect to become water by study of the qualities of oxygen, whereas what is needed is the actual union of the elements.

The two most important of Law's mystical treatises are *An Appeal to all that Doubt*, 1740, and *The Way to Divine Knowledge*, 1752. The first of these should be read by any one desirous of knowing Law's later thought, for it is a clear and fine exposition of his attitude with regard more especially to the nature of man, the unity of all nature, and the quality of fire or desire. The later book is really an account of the main principles of Boehme, with a warning as to the right way to apply them, and it was written as an introduction to the new edition of Boehme's works which Law contemplated publishing.

The following is the aspect of Boehme's teaching which Law most consistently emphasises.

Man was made out of the Breath of God; his soul is a spark of the Deity. It therefore cannot die, for it " has the Unbeginning, Unending Life of God in it." Man has fallen from his high estate through ignorance and inexperience, through seeking separation, taking the part for the whole, desiring the knowledge of good and evil as separate things.

The assertion of self is thus the root of all evil ; for
as soon as the will of man " turns to itself, and would,
as it were, have a Sound of its own, it breaks off
from the divine harmony, and falls into the misery
of its own discord." For it is the state of our will
that makes the state of our life. Hence, by the
" fall," man's standpoint has been dislocated from
centre to circumference, and he lives in a false
imagination. Every quality is equally good, for
there is nothing evil in God from whom all comes ;
but evil appears to be through separation. Thus
strength and desire in the divine nature are necessary and magnificent qualities, but when, as in the
creature, they are separated from love, they appear
as evil.[1] The analogy of the fruit is, in this connection, a favourite one with both Law and Boehme.
When a fruit is unripe (*i.e.* incomplete) it is sour,
bitter, astringent, unwholesome ; but when it has
been longer exposed to the sun and air it becomes
sweet, luscious, and good to eat. Yet it is the
same fruit, and the astringent qualities are not lost
or destroyed, but transmuted and enriched, and
are thus the main cause of its goodness.[2] The only
way to pass from this condition of " bitterness "

[1] This is the idea, essentially mystical, and originating with Boehme,
which is worked out in the suggestive little book, *The Mystery of
Pain*, by James Hinton.

[2] *An Appeal*, *Works*, vol. vi. pp. 27, 28.

to ripeness, from this false imagination to the true one, is the way of death. We must die to what we are before we can be born anew; we must die to the things of this world to which we cling, and for which we desire and hope, and we must turn towards God. This should be the daily, hourly exercise of the mind, until the whole turn and bent of our spirit " points as constantly to God as the needle touched with the loadstone does to the north." [1] To be alive in God, before you are dead to your own nature, is " a thing as impossible in itself, as for a grain of wheat to be alive before it dies."

The root of all, then, is the will or desire. This realisation of the momentous quality of the will is the secret of every religious mystic, the hunger of the soul, as Law calls it, is the first necessity, and all else will follow. [2] It is the seed of everything that can grow in us ; " it is the only workman in nature, and everything is its work ; " it is the true magic power. And this will or desire is always active ; every man's life is a continual state of prayer, and if we are not praying for the things of

---

[1] *The Spirit of Prayer*, *Works*, vol. vii. pp. 23, 24.

[2] *Cf.* St Augustine, " To will God entirely is to have Him " (*City of God*, Book xi. chap. iv.), or Ruysbroek's answer to the priests from Paris who came to consult him on the state of their souls : " You are as you desire to be."

God, we are praying for *something else*.[1] For prayer is but the desire of the soul. Our imaginations and desires are, therefore, the greatest realities we have, and we should look closely to what they are.[2]

It is essential to the understanding of Law, as of Boehme, to remember his belief in the reality and actuality of the oneness of nature and of law.[3] Nature is God's great Book of Revelation, for it is nothing else but God's own outward manifestation of what He inwardly is, and can do. . . . The mysteries of religion, therefore, are no higher, nor deeper than the mysteries of nature.[4] God Himself is subject to this law. There is no question of God's mercy or of His wrath,[5] for it is an eternal principle that we can only receive what we are capable of receiving; and to ask why one person gains no help from the mercy and goodness of God while another does gain help is "like asking why the refreshing dew of heaven does not do that to the flint which it does to the vegetable plant."[6]

Self-denial, or mortification of the flesh is not a thing imposed upon us by the mere will of

[1] See *The Spirit of Prayer*, *Works*, vol. vii. pp. 150, 151.
[2] *An Appeal*, *Works*, vol. vi. p. 169.
[3] *Ibid.*, pp. 19, 20.   [4] *Ibid.*, pp. 69, 80.
[5] *The Spirit of Prayer*, *Works*, vol. vii. pp. 23, 27.
[6] *The Way to Divine Knowledge*, *Works*, vol. vii. p. 60.

God : considered in themselves they have nothing of goodness or holiness, but they have their ground and reason in the nature of the thing, and are as " absolutely necessary to make way for the new birth, as the death of the husk and gross part of the grain is necessary to make way for its vegetable life." [1]

These views are clear enough, but the more mystical ones, such as those which Law and Boehme held, for instance, about fire, can only be understood in the light of this living unity throughout nature, humanity, and divinity.

" Everything in temporal Nature," says Law, " is descended out of that which is eternal, and stands as a palpable, visible Outbirth of it : . . . Fire and Light and Air in this World are not only a true Resemblance of the Holy Trinity in Unity, but are the Trinity itself in its most outward, lowest kind of Existence or Manifestation. . . . Fire compacted, created, separated from Light and Air, is the Elemental Fire of this World : Fire uncreated, uncompacted, unseparated from Light and Air, is the heavenly Fire of Eternity : Fire kindled in any material Thing is only Fire breaking out of its created, compacted state ; it is nothing else but the awakening the Spiritual Properties of that Thing, which being thus stirred up, strive to get rid of that material Creation under which they are imprisoned . . . and were not these spiritual Properties imprisoned in Matter, no material Thing could be made to burn. . . . Fire is not, cannot be a material Thing, it only makes itself visible and sensible by the Destruction of Matter." [2] " If you ask what Fire is in its first true and unbeginning State, not yet entered into any

---

[1] *The Spirit of Prayer*, *Works*, vol. vii. p. 68. See also *ibid.*, pp. 91, 92   [2] *An Appeal*, *Works*, vol. vi. pp. 132, 133.

Creature, It is the Power and Strength, the Glory and Majesty of eternal Nature. . . . If you ask what Fire is in its own spiritual Nature, it is merely a *Desire*, and has no other Nature than that of a *working Desire*, which is continually its *own Kindler*." [1]

All life is a kindled fire in a variety of states, and every dead, insensitive thing is only dead because its fire is quenched or compressed, as in the case of a flint, which is in a state of death ' because its fire is bound, compacted, shut up and imprisoned," but a steel struck against it shows that every particle of the flint consists of this compacted fire.

But even as, throughout all nature, a state of death is an imprisoned fire, so throughout all nature is there only one way of kindling life. You might as well write the word " flame " on the outside of a flint and expect it to emit sparks as to imagine that any speculations of your reason will kindle divine life in your soul.

No : Would you have Fire from a Flint ; its House of Death must be shaken, and its Chains of Darkness broken off by the Strokes of a Steel upon it. This must of all Necessity be done to your Soul, its imprisoned Fire must be awakened by the sharp Strokes of Steel, or no true Light of Life can arise in it.[2]

All life, whether physical or spiritual, means a death to some previous condition, and must be generated in pain.

[1] *An Appeal, Works,* vol. vi. pp. 166.   [2] *Ibid.,* p. 82.

If this mystical view of Fire be clear, it will be easy enough to follow what Law says about Light and Darkness, or Air, Water, and Earth, interpreting them all in the same way as " eternal Things become gross, finite, measurable, divisible, and transitory." [1]

The Spirit of Prayer is of all Law's works the one most steeped in mystic ardour, and it possesses a charm, a melody of rhythm, and an imaginative quality rarely to be found in his earlier work. It should be read by those who would see Law under a little known aspect, and who do not realise that we have an English mystic who expresses, with a strength and beauty which Plotinus himself has rarely surpassed, the longing of the soul for union with the Divine.

Burke, Coleridge, and Carlyle are three very different writers who are alike in the mystical foundations of their belief, and who, through their writings, for over a hundred years in England carry on the mystical attitude and diffuse much mystical thought.

Burke, the greatest and most philosophic of English statesmen, was so largely because of his mystic spirit and imagination. Much of the greatness of his political pamphlets and speeches and of their enduring value is owing to the fact that his argu-

[1] *An Appeal, Works,* vol. vi. p. 115.

ments are based on a sense of oneness and continuity, of oneness in the social organism and of continuity in the spirit which animates it. He believes in a life in the Universe, in a divine order, mysterious and inscrutable in origins and in ends, of which man and society are a part.

This society is linked together in mutual service from the lowest to the highest. " Society is indeed a contract," he says in a memorable passage,

It is a partnership in all science ; a partnership in all art ; a partnership in every virtue, and in all perfection. As the ends of such a partnership cannot be obtained in many generations, it becomes a partnership not only between those who are living, but between those who are living, those who are dead, and those who are to be born. Each contract of each particular state is but a clause in the great primæval contract of eternal society, linking the lower with the higher natures, connecting the visible and invisible world, according to a fixed compact sanctioned by the inviolable oath which holds all physical and all moral natures, each in their appointed place.

These are strange words for an English statesman to address to the English public in the year 1790 ; the thought they embody seems more in keeping with its surroundings when we hear it thundered out anew forty years later by the raw Scotch preacher-philosopher in the chapter he calls " Organic Filaments " in his odd but strangely stirring mystical rhapsody, *Sartor Resartus*.

It is on this belief of oneness, this interrelationship

and interdependence that all Burke's deepest practical wisdom is based. It is on this he makes
his appeal for high principle and noble example
to the great families with hereditary trusts and
fortunes, who, he says, he looks on as the great
oaks that shade a country and perpetuate their
benefits from generation to generation.

This imaginative belief in the reality of a central spiritual life is always accompanied, whether
definitely expressed or not, with a belief in the
value of particulars, of the individual, as opposed
to general statements and abstract philosophy.
The mystic, who believes in an inward moulding
spirit, necessarily believes that all reforms must
come from within, and that, as Burke points out
in the *Present Discontents*, good government depends
not upon laws but upon individuals. Blake, in a
characteristic phrase, says : " He who would do
good to another must do it in minute particulars ;
general good is the plea of the hypocrite, flatterer,
and scoundrel." This sums up the essence of the
social philosophy of these three thinkers, as seen
by Burke's insistence on the value of concrete details, in Coleridge's use of them in his Lay Sermon,
and in Carlyle's belief in the importance of the single
individual life in history.

It is easy to see that Coleridge's attitude of
mind and the main lines of his philosophy were

mystical. From early years, as we know from Lamb, he was steeped in the writings of the Neo-platonists, and these, together with Boehme, in whom he was much interested, and Schelling, strengthened a type of belief already natural to him.

In spite of his devotion to the doctrines of Hartley, it is clear from his poetry and letters, that Coleridge very early had doubts concerning the adequacy of the intellect as an instrument for arriving at truth, and that at the same time the conviction was slowly gaining ground with him that an act of the will is necessary in order to bring man into contact with reality. Coleridge believed in a Spirit of the universe with which man could come into contact, both directly by desire, and also mediately through the forms and images of nature, and in the *Religious Musings* (1794) we get very early a statement of this mystical belief.

> There is one Mind, one omnipresent Mind
> Omnific. His most holy name is Love.

From Him—

> . . . we roam unconscious, or with hearts
> Unfeeling of our universal Sire,

and the greatest thing we can achieve, " our noon-tide majesty," is—

> to know ourselves
> Parts and proportions of one wonderous whole !

The way to attain this knowledge is not by a process of reasoning, but by a definite act of will, when the " drowséd soul " begins to feel dim recollections of its nobler nature, and so gradually becomes attracted and absorbed to perfect love—

> and centered there
> God only to behold, and know, and feel,
> Till by exclusive consciousness of God
> All self-annihilated it shall make
> God its Identity : God all in all !

This sense of " oneness," with the desire to reach out to it, was very strong with Coleridge in these earlier years, and he writes to Thelwall in 1797, " The universe itself, what but an immense heap of little things ? . . . My mind feels as if it ached to behold and know something *great*, something *one* and *indivisible*." He is ever conscious of the symbolic quality of all things by which we are visibly surrounded,

> all that meets the bodily sense I deem
> Symbolical, one mighty alphabet
> For infant minds.[1]

To pierce through the outer covering, and realise

---

[1] *The Destiny of Nations*, ll. 16-18.

the truth which they embody, it is necessary to
feel as well as to see, and it is the loss of this power
of feeling which Coleridge deplores in those bitterly
sad lines in the *Dejection Ode* when he gazes " with
how blank an eye " at the starry heavens, and
cries,

> I see, not feel, how beautiful they are !

It is in this Ode that we find the most complete
description in English verse of that particular
state of depression and stagnation which often
follows on great exaltation, and to which the religious mystics have given the name of the " dark
night of the soul." This is an experience, not
common to all mystics, but very marked in some,
who, like St John of the Cross and Madame Guyon,
are intensely devotional and ecstatic. It seems
to be a well-defined condition of listlessness, apathy,
and *dryness*, as they call it, not a state of active
pain, but of terrible inertia, weariness, and incapa-
city for feeling ; " a wan and heartless mood,"
says Coleridge,

> A grief without a pang, void, dark, and drear,
> A stifled, drowsy, unimpassioned grief,
> Which finds no natural outlet, no relief,
> In word, or sigh, or tear.

Coleridge's distrust of the intellect as sole guide,

and his belief in some kind of intuitional act being necessary to the apprehension of reality, which he felt as early as 1794, was strengthened by his study of the German transcendental philosophers, and in March 1801 he writes, " My opinion is that deep thinking is attainable only by a man of deep feeling ; and that all truth is a species of Revelation."

Coleridge, following Kant, gave the somewhat misleading name of " reason " (as opposed to ' understanding ") to the intuitive power by which man apprehends God directly, and, in his view, imagination is the faculty, which in the light of this intuitive reason interprets and unifies the symbols of the natural world. Hence its value, for it alone gives man the key

> Of that eternal language, which thy God
> Utters, who from eternity doth teach
> Himself in all, and all things in himself.[1]

Carlyle's mysticism is the essence of his being, it flames through his amazing medley of writings, it guides his studies and his choice of subjects, it unifies and explains his visions, his thought, and his doctrines. His is a mystical attitude and belief of a perfectly simple and broad kind, including no abstruse subtleties of metaphysical speculation,

[1] *Frost at Midnight*, ll. 60-62.

as with Coleridge, but based on one or two deeply
rooted convictions. This position seems to have
been reached by him partly through intellectual
conflict which found relief and satisfaction in the
view of life taken by Goethe, Fichte, and other
German " transcendental " thinkers ; but partly
also through a definite psychical experience which
befell him in Edinburgh when he was twenty-six,
and which from that day changed for him the
whole of his outlook on life. He speaks of it
himself as " a Spiritual New-birth, or Baphometic
Fire-baptism." It came to him after a period
of great wretchedness, of torture with doubt and
despair, and—what is significant—" during three
weeks of total sleeplessness." These are conditions
which would be likely to reduce his body to the
state of weakness and sensitiveness which seems
often antecedent to psychic experience. He has
given an account of the incident in *Sartor* (Book ii.
chap. vii.), when, he says, " there rushed like a
stream of fire over my whole soul ; and I shook
base Fear away from me for ever. I was strong,
of unknown strength ; a spirit, almost a god."
The revelation seems to have been of the nature
of a certainty and assertion of his own inherent
divinity, his " native God-created majesty," freedom
and potential greatness. This brought with it a
characteristic defiance of untoward outer circum-

stances which gave him strength and resolution. "Perhaps," he says, " I directly thereupon began to be a man."

Carlyle believes that the world and everything in it is the expression of one great indivisible Force ; that nothing is separate, nothing is dead or lost, but that all " is borne forward on the bottomless, shoreless flood of Action, and lives through perpetual metamorphoses." Everything in the world is an embodiment of this great Force, this " Divine Idea," hence everything is important and charged with meaning. " Rightly viewed no meanest object is insignificant ; all objects are as windows, through which the philosophic eye looks into Infinitude itself." [1]

The universe is thus the " living visible garment of God," and " matter exists only spiritually," " to represent some Idea, and *body* it forth." We, each of us, are therefore one expression of this central spirit, the only abiding Reality ; and so, in turn, everything we know and see is but an envelope or clothing encasing something more vital which is invisible within. Just as books are the most miraculous things men can make, because a book " is the *purest* embodiment a Thought of man can have," so great men are the highest embodiment of Divine Thought visible to us here.

[1] *Sartor Resartus*, Book i. chap. xi.

Great men are, as it were, separate phrases, " inspired texts " of the great book of revelation, perpetually interpreting and unfolding in various ways the Godlike to man (*Hero as Man of Letters*, and *Sartor*, Book ii. chap. viii.).

From this ground-belief spring all Carlyle's views and aims. Hence his gospel of hero-worship, for the " hero " is the greatest embodied " Idea " a man can know, he is a " living light fountain," he is " a man sent hither to make the divine mystery more impressively known to us." Hence it is clear that the first condition of the great man is that he should be sincere, that he should *believe*. " The merit of originality is not novelty : it is sincerity. The believing man is the original man." It is equally necessary that his admirers should be sincere, they too must believe, and not only, as Coleridge puts it, " believe that they believe." No more immoral act can be done by a human creature, says Carlyle, than to pretend to believe and worship when he does not.

Hence also springs Carlyle's doctrine of work. If man is but the material embodiment of a spiritual Idea or Force, then his clear duty is to express that Force within him to the utmost of his power. It is what he is here for, and only so can he bring help and light to his fellow-men.[1]   And

[1] See *Sartor*, Book iii. chap. iv.

Carlyle, with Browning, believes that it is not the actual deeds accomplished that matter, no man may judge of these, for " man is the spirit he worked in ; not what he did, but what he became."

CHAPTER V

DEVOTIONAL AND RELIGIOUS MYSTICS

ALL mystics are devotional and all are religious in the truest sense of the terms. Yet it seems legitimate to group under this special heading those writers whose views are expressed largely in the language of the Christian religion, as is the case with our earliest mystics, with Crashaw and Francis Thompson, and it applies in . some measure to Blake. But beyond this, it seems, in more general terms, to apply specially to those who are so conscious of God that they seem to live in His presence, and who are chiefly concerned with approaching Him, not by way of Love, Beauty, Wisdom, or Nature, but directly, through purgation and adoration.

This description, it is obvious, though it fits fairly well the other writers here included, by no means suffices for Blake. For he possessed in addition a philosophy, a system, and a profound scheme of the universe revealed to him in vision. But within what category could Blake be imprisoned? He outsoars them all and includes them all. We can only say that the dominant impression he leaves with us that is of his vivid, intimate consciousness of the Divine presence and his attitude of devotion.

We have seen that the earliest mystical thought came into this country by way of the writings of " Dionysius " and of the Victorines (Hugh and Richard of St Victor), and it is this type of thought and belief cast into the mould of the Catholic Church that we find mainly in the little group of early English mystics, whose writings date from the middle of the thirteenth to the beginning of the fifteenth century.[1]

These early Catholic mystics are interesting from a psychological point of view, and they are often subtle exponents of the deepest mystical truths and teachings, and in some cases this is combined with great literary power and beauty.

One of the earliest examples of this thought in English literature is the tender and charming lyric by Thomas de Hales, written probably before 1240. Here is perhaps the first expression in our poetry of passionate yearning of the soul towards Christ as her true lover, and of the joy of mystic union with Him. A maid of Christ, says the poet, has begged him to " wurche a luve ron " (make a love-song), which he does ; and points out to her that this world's love is false and fickle, and

---

[1] The mystical desire for close contact with God is expressed in English as early as before 1170, in Godric's song to the Virgin.

that worldly lovers shall pass away like a wind's
blast.

> Hwer is Paris and Heleyne
>> That weren so bright and feyre on bleo :
> Amadas, Tristram and Dideyne
>> Yseudé and allé theo:
> Ector with his scharpé meyne
>> And Cesar riche of wor[l]des feo ?
> Heo beoth iglyden ut of the reyne,
>> So the schef is of the cleo.

As the corn from the hill-side, Paris and Helen
and all bright lovers have passed away, and it is
as if they had never lived.

But, maid, if you want a lover, he continues, I
can direct you to one, the fairest, truest, and richest
in the whole world. Henry, King of England, is
his vassal, and to thee, maid, this lover sends a
message and desires to know thee.

> Mayde to the he send his sonde
> And wilneth for to beo the cuth.

And so the poem goes on to express in simple
terms of earthly love, the passionate delight and joy
and peace of the soul in attaining to union with her
God, in whose dwelling is perfect bliss and safety.

This poem is a delicate example of what is called
" erotic mysticism," that is the love and attraction
of the soul for God, and of God for the soul, expressed
in the terms of the love between man and woman.
It is a type of expression characteristic of the

great mystics of the Catholic Church, especially in the Middle Ages,[1] and we find a good deal of it in our earliest mystical writers. One of the most charming examples of it other than this lyric, is the chapter " Of Love " in the *Ancren Riwle*, or Rule for Anchoresses, written probably early in the thirteenth century. An account is there given, quite unsurpassed for delicate beauty, of the wooing of the soul by God.[2] On the whole, however, this type of mysticism is rare in England, and we scarcely meet it again after these early writers until we come to the poems of Crashaw. The finest expression of it is the Song of Solomon, and it is easy to see that such a form of symbolism is specially liable to degradation, and is open to grave dangers, which it has not always escaped. Yet, in no other terms known to man is it possible so fully to express the sense of insatiable craving and desire as well as the rapture of intimate communion felt by the mystic towards his God, as in the language of that great passion which, in its purest form, is the best thing known to man and his highest glory. " I saw Him, and sought Him, I had Him and I wanted Him." Could any words more completely express the infinity of love's desire, ever unsatisfied even in

[1] See *Mysticism*, by E. Underhill, pp. 162-166.

[2] *The Ancren Riwle*, ed. J. Morton, Camden Society, 1853, pp. 397-403.

possession, than does this love-cry from the heart of Julian the anchoress of Norwich ?

The intensity and freshness of religious feeling of a mystical type in England in the twelfth, thirteenth, and fourteenth centuries are often not realised, partly owing to the fact that much of the religious writing of this time is still in manuscript. The country was full of devotees who had taken religious vows, which they fulfilled either in the many monasteries and convents, or often in single cells, as " hermit " or " anchoress." Here they lived a life devoted to contemplation and prayer, and to the spiritual assistance of those who sought them out.

The hermits, of whom there were a large number, were apparently free to move from one neighbourhood to another, but the woman recluse, or " anchoress," seldom or never left the walls of her cell, a little house of two or three rooms built generally against the church wall, so that one of her windows could open into the church, and another, veiled by a curtain, looked on to the outer world, where she held converse with and gave counsel to those who came to see her. Sometimes a little group of recluses lived together, like those three sisters of Dorsetshire for whom the *Ancren Riwle* was written, a treatise which gives us so many homely details of this type of life.

Richard Rolle (c. 1300-1349), of Hampole, near Doncaster, and the Lady Julian, a Benedictine nun of Norwich (1342-c.1413), are the two most interesting examples of the mediæval recluse in England. Both seem to have had a singular charm of character and a purity of mystical devotion which has impressed itself on their writings. Richard Rolle, who entered upon a hermit's life at nineteen, on leaving Oxford, had great influence both through his life and work on the whole group of fourteenth-century religious writers, and so on the thought of mediæval England. His contemporaries thought him mad, they jeered at him and abused him, but he went quietly on his way, preaching and writing. Love forced him to write ; love, he said, gave him wisdom and subtlety, and he preached a religion of love. Indeed the whole of his work is a symphony of feeling, a song of Love, and forms a curious reaction against the exaltation of reason and logic in scholasticism. He wrote a large number of treatises and poems, both in Latin and English, lyrical songs and alliterative homilies, burning spiritual rhapsodies and sound practical sermons, all of which were widely known and read. Certain points about Rolle are of special interest and distinguish him from other mystics and seers. One is that for him the culminating mystical experience took the form of melody, rhythm, harmony. He is the most musical of mystics, and where others " see " or " feel " Reality, he " hears " it. Hence his description of his soul's adventures is peculiarly beautiful, he thinks in images and symbols of music, and in his writings we find some of the most exquisite passages in the whole literature of mysticism, veritable songs of spiritual joy. In the *Fire of Love*, perhaps the finest of his more mystical works, he traces in detail his journey along the upward path. This is very individual, and it differs in some important respects from other similar records. He passed through the stage of " purgation," of struggle between the flesh and spirit, of penitence and aspiration, through " illumination," until he reached, after nearly three years, the third stage of contemplation of God through love.[1]

In this condition, after about a year, " the door of heaven yet biding open," he experienced the three phases to which he gives the names of " calor, canor, dulcor," heat, song, and sweetness. " Heat soothly I call when the mind truly is kindled in Love Everlasting, and the heart on the same manner to burn not hopingly, but verily is felt." [2]

This " burning " seems to have been for him a real physical sensation, a bodily condition induced

[1] *Fire of Love*, Bk. i. cap. xvi. p. 36.
[2] *Ibid.*, Bk. i. cap. xv. p. 33.

by the adventure of the spirit. This is not unusual in mystical states, and possibly the cryptic notes made by Pascal record a similar experience.[1] He continued in this warmth for nine months, when suddenly he felt and heard the " canor," the " spiritual music," the " invisible melody " of heaven. Here is his description of his change from " burning love " to the state of " songful love."

Whilst . . . I sat in chapel, in the night, before supper, as I my psalms sung, as it were the sound of readers or rather singers about me I beheld. Whilst also, praying to heaven, with all desire I took heed, suddenly, in what manner I wot not, in me the sound of song I felt ; and likeliest heavenly melody I took, with me dwelling in mind. Forsooth my thought continually to mirth of song was changed : and as it were the same that loving I had thought, and in prayers and psalms had said, the same in sound I showed, and so forth with [began] to sing that [which] before I had said, and from plenitude of inward sweetness I burst forth, privily indeed, alone before my Maker.[2]

The sweetness of this inward spiritual song is beyond any sound that may be heard with bodily ears, even lovers can only catch snatches of it. " Worldly lovers soothly words or ditties of our song may know, for the words they read : but the tone and sweetness of that song they may not learn." [3] The final stage of " sweetness " seems really to include the other two, it is their completion

[1] See *Mysticism*, by E. Underhill, pp. 228, 229.
[2] *Fire of Love*, Bk. i. cap. xvi. p. 36.
[3] *Ibid.*, Bk. ii. cap. iii. and xii.

and fruition. The first two, says Rolle, are gained
by devotion, and out of them springs the third.[1]
Rolle's description of it, of the all-pervading holy
joy, rhythm, and melody, when the soul, " now
become as it were a living pipe," is caught up
into the music of the spheres, " and in the sight of
God . . . joying sounds,"[2] deserves to be placed
beside what is perhaps the most magnificent passage in all mystical literature, where Plotinus tells
us of the choral dance of the soul about her
God.[3]

Enough has been said to show that Rolle is a
remarkable individual, and one of the most poetic
of the English religious mystical writers, and it is
regrettable that some of his other works are not
more easily accessible. Unfortunately, the poem
with which his name is generally associated, *The
Pricke of Conscience*, is entirely unlike all his other
work, both in form and matter. It is a long,
prosaic and entirely unmystical homily in riming
couplets, of a very ordinary mediæval type, stirring
men's minds to the horrors of sin by dwelling on
the pains of purgatory and hell. It would seem
almost certain, on internal evidence, that the same
hand cannot have written it and the *Fire of Love*,
and recent investigation appears to make it clear

[1] *Fire of Love*, Bk. i. cap. xv.   [2] *Ibid.*, Bk. ii. cap. vii.
[3] *Enneads*, vi. §§ 8, 9.

that Rolle's part in it, if any, was merely of the
nature of compilation or translation of some other
work, possibly by Grosseteste.[1]

Of the life of the Lady Julian we know very little,
except that she was almost certainly a Benedictine
nun, and that she lived for many years in an anchoress's cell close to the old church of St Julian at
Conisford, near Norwich. But her character and
charm are fully revealed in the little book she has
left of *Revelations of Divine Love*, which contains
a careful account of a definite psychological experience through which she passed on the 8th day of
May 1373, when she was thirty years of age. She
adds to this record of fact certain commentaries
and explanations which, she says, have been taught
her gradually in the course of the subsequent twenty
years. This experience, which lasted altogether between five and six hours, was preceded by a seven
days' sickness most vividly described, ending in a
semi-rigidity of the body as if it were already half
dead, and it took the form of sixteen " Shewings "
or " Visions." These, she says, reached her in
three ways, " by bodily sight, by word formed
in mine understanding " (verbal messages which
took form in her mind), " and by spiritual sight."
But of this last, she adds, " I may never fully tell

[1] See *The Authorship of the Prick of Conscience*, by H. E. Allen,
Radcliffe College Monographs, No. 15, Ginn and Co., 1910.

it." [1]   It is impossible here to do justice to this little
book, for it is one of the most important documents
in the history of mysticism.   There is no mention in
it of any preliminary " purgative " stage, nor of
any ultimate experience of ecstasy ; it is simply—
if one may so put it—a narrative of certain intimate
talks with God, once granted, when, during a few
hours of the writer's life, He explained various
difficulties and made clear to her certain truths.
The impression left of the nearness of God to the
soul was so vivid and sustaining, that it is not
possible to read the record of it, even now, across
six hundred years, without feeling strangely stirred
by the writer's certainty and joy.

Her vision is of Love : Love is its meaning, and
it was shown her for Love ; she sees that God is Love
and that God and man are one.   " God is nearer
to us than our own soul, for man is God, and God
is in all.   If we could only know ourselves, our
trouble would be cleared away, but it is easier to
come to the knowing of God than to know our own
soul.[2]   " Our passing life here that we have in our

[1] *Revelations*, ed. Warrack, pp. 21, 178.   All the quotations which
follow are taken from this edition of the *Revelations*.

[2] *Revelations*, p. 135.   It is interesting to compare the words
of other mystics upon this point ; as for instance Richard of St
Victor in *Benjamin Minor*, cap. 75, or Walter Hylton in *The Scale
of Perfection*.   Note the emphasis laid upon it by Wordsworth, who
indicates self-knowledge as the mark of those who have attained
the " unitive " stage; see p. 66 above.

sense-soul knoweth not what our Self is," and the cause of our disease is that we rest in little things which can never satisfy us, for " our Soul may never have rest in things that are beneath itself." She actually saw God enfolding all things. " For as the body is clad in the cloth, and the flesh in the skin, and the bones in the flesh, and the heart in the whole, so are we, soul and body, clad in the Goodness of God, and enclosed." She further had sight of all things that are made, and her description of this " Shewing " is so beautiful and characteristic that it must be given in her own words.

" In this same time our Lord shewed me a spiritual sight of His homely loving. . . . He shewed me a little thing, the quantity of an hazel-nut, in the palm of my hand ; and it was as round as a ball. I looked thereupon with the eye of my understanding, and thought : *What may this be ?* And it was answered generally thus : *It is all that is made.* I marvelled how it might last, for methought it might suddenly have fallen to naught for little[ness]. And I was answered in my understanding : *It lasteth, and ever shall [last] for that God loveth it.* And so All-thing hath the Being by the love of God." Later, she adds, "Well I wot that heaven and earth, and all that is made is great and large, fair and good ; but the cause why it shewed so little to my sight was for that I saw it in the presence of Him that is the Maker of all things : for to a soul that seeth the Maker of all, all that is made seemeth full little." " In this Little Thing," she continues, " I saw three properties. The first is that God made it, the second is that God loveth it, the third, that God keepeth it. But what is to me verily the Maker, the Keeper, and the Lover—I cannot tell; for till I am Substantially oned to Him,

I may never have full rest nor very bliss : that is to say, till I be so fastened to Him, that there is right nought that is made betwixt my God and me " (*Revelations*, pp. 10, 18).

Julian's vision with regard to sin is of special interest. The problem of evil has never been stated in terser or more dramatic form.

After this I saw God in a Point, that is to say, in mine under-standing,—by which sight I saw that He is in all things. I beheld and considered, seeing and knowing in sight, with a soft dread, and thought : *What is sin* ? (*Ibid*, p. 26).

Here is the age-old difficulty. God, so the mystic sees, is " in the Mid-point of all thing," and yet, as Julian says, it is " certain He doeth no sin." The solution given to her is that " sin is no deed," it " hath no part of being," and it can only be known by the pain it is cause of. Sin is a negation, a failure, an emptiness of love, but pain *is* some-thing, it is a purification. Sin brings with it pain, " to me was shewed no harder hell than sin " ; but we must go through the pain in order to learn, without it we could never have the bliss. As a wave draws back from the shore, in order to return again with fuller force ; so sin, the lack of love, is permitted for a time, in order that an opening be made for an inrush of the Divine Love, fuller and more complete than would otherwise be possible. It is in some such way as this, dimly shadowed, that it was shown to Julian that sin and pain are necessary parts of the scheme of God. Hence God does not blame us for sin, for it brings its own blame or punishment with it, nay more, " sin shall be no shame to man, but worship," a bold saying, which none but a mystic would dare utter. When God seeth our sin, she says, and our despair in pain, " His love excuseth us, and of His great courtesy He doeth away all our blame, and beholdeth us with ruth and pity as children innocent and unloathful."

It would be pleasant to say more of Julian, but perhaps her own words have sufficed to show that here we are dealing with one of the great mystics of the world. Childlike and yet rashly bold, deeply spiritual, yet intensely human, " a simple creature, unlettered," yet presenting solutions of problems which have racked humanity, she inherits the true paradoxical nature of the mystic, to which is added a beauty and delicacy of thought and expression all her own.

There were many other mystical works written about this time in England. Of these the best known and the finest is *The Scale, or Ladder, of Perfection*, by Walter Hylton, the Augustinian, and head of a house of canons at Thurgarton, near Newark, who died in 1396. This is a practical and scientific treatise of great beauty on the spiritual life.[1] An interesting group of writings are the five little treatises, almost certainly by one author (c. 1350-1400), to be found in Harleian 674, and other MSS. Their names are *The Cloud of Unknowing*, *The Epistle of Prayer*, *The Epistle of Discretion*, *The Treatise of Discerning Spirits*, and *The Epistle of Privy Counsel*. We find here for the first time in English the influence and spirit of Dionysius, and it is probably to the same unknown writer we owe the first (very free) translation of the *Mystical Theology* of Dionysius, *Deonise Hid Divinite*, which is bound up with these other manuscripts.

These little tracts are written by a practical mystic, one who was able to describe with peculiar accuracy and vividness the physical and psychological sensations accompanying mystical initiation. *The Cloud of Unknowing* is an application in simple English of the Dionysian teaching of concentration joined to the practice of contemplation taught by Richard of St Victor, and it describes very clearly the preliminary struggles and bewilderment of the soul. The *Epistle of Privy Counsel* (still in MS.) is the most advanced in mystical teaching : the writer in it tries to explain very intimately the nature of " onehede with God," and to give instruction

---

[1] Dr Inge gives an excellent detailed account of it in *Studies of English Mystics*, 1906, pp. 80-123.

in simple and yet deeply subtle terms as to the means for attaining this.

There is a mystical strain in other writings of this time, the most notable from the point of view of literature being in the fourteenth-century alliterative poem of *Piers the Plowman*.[1] This is mystical throughout in tone, more especially in the idea of the journey of the soul in search of Truth, only to find, after many dangers and disciplines and adventures, that—

> If grace graunte the to go in this wise,
> Thow shalt see in thi-selve Treuthe sitte in thine herte
> In a cheyne of charyte as thow a childe were.[2]

Moreover, the vision of Dowel, Dobet, and Dobest, bears a definite analogy to the three stages of the mystic's path, as will be seen if the description of the qualities of these three are examined, as they are given in B., Passus viii. ll. 78-102.

Crashaw, George Herbert, and Christopher Harvey all alike sound the personal note in their religious poems. All three writers describe the love of the soul for God in the terms of passionate human love : Crashaw with an ardour which has never been surpassed, Herbert with a homely intimacy quite peculiar to him, and Christopher Harvey with a point and epigrammatic setting

---

[1] See *Piers Plowman*, by J. J. Jusserand, 1894.
[2] B., Passus v., 614-616.

which serve only to enhance the deep feeling of the thought.

In many a lyric of flaming passion Crashaw expresses his love-longing for his God, and he describes in terms only matched by his spiritual descendant, Francis Thompson, the desire of God to win the human soul.

> Let not my Lord, the mighty lover
> Of soules, disdain that I discover
>   The hidden art
> Of his high stratagem to win your heart,
>   It was his heavnly art
>   Kindly to crosse you
>   In your mistaken love,
>   That, at the next remove
>   Thence he might tosse you
>   And strike your troubled heart
>   Home to himself.[1]

The main feature of Herbert's poetry is the religious love lyric, the cry of the individual soul to God. This is the mystical quality in his verse, which is quieter and far less musical than Crashaw's, but which possesses at times a tender fragrance and freshness, as in the little poem *Love*.

Christopher Harvey, the friend of Izaak Walton and the admirer of Herbert, has in his poems some lines which breathe almost as rapturous a passion of spiritual love as anything in Crashaw.

[1] *Poems*, ed. Waller, 1904, p. 283.

Such is his epigram on the *Insatiableness of the Heart.*

> The whole round world is not enough to fill
> The heart's three corners ; but it craveth still.
> Onely the Trinity, that made it, can
> Suffice the vast-triangled heart of man.[1]

Or again, in a later epigram in the same poem (*The School of the Heart*), he puts the main teaching of Plotinus and of all mystics into four pregnant lines—

> My busie stirring heart, that seekes the best,
> Can find no place on earth wherein to rest ;
> For God alone, the Author of its blisse,
> Its only rest, its onely center is.

But it is Crashaw who, of these three, shares in fullest measure the passion of the great Catholic mystics, and more especially of St Teresa, whom he seems almost to have worshipped. His hymn to her " name and honor " is one of the great English poems ; it burns with spiritual flame, it soars with noble desire. Near the beginning of it, Crashaw has, in six simple lines, pictured the essential mystic attitude of action, not necessarily or consciously accompanied by either a philosophy or a theology. He is speaking of Teresa's childish

[1] *Poems*, ed. Grosart, 1874, p. 134.

attempt to run away and become a martyr among
the Moors.

> She never undertook to know
> What death with love should have to doe ;
> Nor has she e're yet understood
> Why to shew love, she should shed blood
> Yet though she cannot tell you why,
> She can LOVE, and she can DY.

Spiritual love has never been more rapturously
sung than in this marvellous hymn. Little wonder
that it haunted Coleridge's memory, and that its
deep emotion and rich melody stimulated his poet's
ear and imagination to write *Christabel*.[1] Crashaw's
influence also on Patmore, more especially on the
Sponsa Dei, as well as later on Francis Thompson,
is unmistakable.

William Blake is one of the great mystics of the
world ; and he is by far the greatest and most profound who has spoken in English. Like Henry
More and Wordsworth, he lived in a world of glory,
of spirit and of vision, which, for him, was the only
real world. At the age of four he saw God looking in at the window, and from that time until he
welcomed the approach of death by singing songs
of joy which made the rafters ring, he lived in an
atmosphere of divine illumination. The material
facts of his career were simple and uneventful.

[1] See *Additional Table Talk of S. T. C.*, ed. T. Ashe, 1884, p. 322.

He was an engraver by profession, poet and painter by choice, mystic and seer by nature. From the outer point of view his life was a failure. He was always crippled by poverty, almost wholly unappreciated in the world of art and letters of his day, consistently misunderstood even by his best friends, and pronounced mad by those who most admired his work. Yet, like all true mystics, he was radiantly happy and serene ; rich in the midst of poverty. For he lived and worked in a world, and amongst a company, little known of ordinary men :—

> With a blue sky spread over with wings,
> And a mild Sun that mounts & sings ;
> With trees & fields full of Fairy elves,
> And little devils who fight for themselves—
>
> •   •   •   •   •
>
> With Angels planted in Hawthorn bowers,
> And God Himself in the passing hours.[1]

It is not surprising that he said, in speaking of Lawrence and other popular artists who sometimes patronisingly visited him, " They pity me, but 'tis they are the just objects of pity, I possess my visions and peace. They have bartered their birthright for a mess of pottage." The strength of his illumination at times intoxicated him with joy, as he writes to Hayley (October 23, 1804) after a recurrence of vision which had lapsed for some

[1] *Poems*, ed. Sampson, p. 305.

years, "Dear Sir, excuse my enthusiasm or rather madness, for I am really drunk with intellectual vision whenever I take a pencil or graver into my hand." This is the "divine madness" of which Plato speaks, the "inebriation of Reality," the ecstasy which makes the poet ",drunk with life." [1]

In common with other mystics, with Boehme, St Teresa, and Madame Guyon, Blake claimed that much of his work was written under direct inspiration, that it was an automatic composition, which, whatever its source, did not come from the writer's normal consciousness. In speaking of the prophetic book *Milton*, he says—

I have written this poem from immediate dictation, twelve or sometimes twenty or thirty lines at a time, without pre-meditation and even against my will. The time it has taken in writing was thus rendered non-existent, and an immense poem exists which seems to be the labour of a long life, all produced without labour or study.

Whatever may be their source, all Blake's writings are deeply mystical in thought, and symbolic in expression, and this is true of the (apparently) simple little *Songs of Innocence*, no less than of the great, and only partially intelligible, prophetic books. To deal at all adequately with these works, with the thought and teaching they contain, and

[1] See *Mysticism*, by E. Underhill, pp. 282-286, and specially the passage from the *Fioretti* of St Francis of Assisi, chap. xlviii., quoted on p. 285.

the method of clothing it, would necessitate a volume, if not a small library, devoted to that purpose. It is possible, however, to indicate certain fundamental beliefs and assertions which lie at the base of Blake's thought and of his very unusual attitude towards life, and which, once grasped, make clear a large part of his work. It must be remembered that these assertions were for him not matters of belief, but of passionate knowledge—he was as sure of them as of his own existence.

Blake founds his great myth on his perception of unity at the heart of things expressing itself in endless diversity. " God is in the lowest effects as [in] the highest causes. He is become a worm that he may nourish the weak. . . . Everything on earth is the word of God, and in its essence is God." [1]

In the *Everlasting Gospel*, Blake emphasises, with more than his usual amount of paradox, the inherent divinity of man. God, speaking to Christ as the highest type of humanity, says—

> If thou humblest thyself, thou humblest me.
> Thou also dwellst in Eternity.
> Thou art a man : God is no more :
> Thy own humanity learn to adore,
> For that is my Spirit of Life. [2]

---

[1] Notes to Lavater.

[2] From version γ2 in *Poetical Works*, ed. John Sampson, 1905, p. 253.

Similarly the union of man with God is the whole gist of that apparently most chaotic of the prophetic books, *Jerusalem*.

The proof of the divinity of man, it would seem, lies in the fact that he desires God, for he cannot desire what he has not seen. This view is summed up in the eight sentences which form the little book (about 2 inches long by 1½ inches broad) in the British Museum, *Of Natural Religion*. Here are four of them.

Man's perceptions are not bounded by organs of perception, he perceives more than sense (tho' ever so acute) can discover.

None could have other than natural or organic thoughts if he had none but organic perceptions.

Man's desires are limited by his perceptions, none can desire what he has not perceiv'd.

The desires and perceptions of man untaught by anything but organs of sense, must be limited to objects of sense.

The solution of the difficulty is given in large script on the last of the tiny pages of the volume :

Therefore God becomes as we are, that we may be as he is.

According to Blake, the universe as we know it, is the result of the fall of the one life from unity into division. This fall has come about through man seeking separation, and taking the part for the whole. (See Jacob Boehme's view, pp. 94, 95 above, which is identical with that of Blake.) " Nature," therefore, or the present form of mental existence, is the result of a contraction of consciousness or " selfhood," a tendency for everything to shrink and contract about its own centre. This condition or " state " Blake personifies as " Urizen " (= Reason) a great dramatic figure who stalks through the prophetic books, proclaiming himself " God from Eternity to Eternity," taking up now one characteristic and now another, but ever of the nature of materialism, opaqueness, contraction. In the case of man, the result of this contraction is to close him up into separate " selfhoods," so that the inlets of communication with the universal spirit have become gradually stopped up ; until now, for most men, only the five senses (one of the least of the many possible channels of communication) are available for the uses of the natural world. Blake usually refers to this occurrence as the " flood " : that is, the rush of general belief in the five senses that overwhelmed or submerged the knowledge of all other channels of wisdom, except such arts as were saved, which are symbolised under the names of Noah (= Imagination) and his sons. He gives a fine account of this in *Europe* (p. 8), beginning—

> Plac'd in the order of the stars, when the five senses whelm'd
> In deluge o'er the earth-born man, then turn'd the fluxile eyes
> Into two stationary orbs, concentrating all things.

The ever-varying spiral ascents to the heavens of heavens
Were bended downward, and the nostrils' golden gates shut,
Turn'd outward, barr'd, and petrify'd against the infinite.

The only way out of this self-made prison is
through the Human Imagination, which is thus
the Saviour of the world. By "Imagination"
Blake would seem to mean all that we include
under sympathy, insight, idealism, and vision, as
opposed to self-centredness, logical argument, materialism, and concrete, scientific fact. For him,
Imagination is the one great reality, in it alone
he sees a human faculty that touches both nature
and spirit, thus uniting them in one. The language
of Imagination is Art, for it speaks through symbols, so that men shut up in their selfhoods are
thus ever reminded that nature herself is a symbol.
When this is once fully realised, we are freed from
the delusion imposed upon us from without by
the seemingly fixed reality of external things. If
we consider all material things as symbols, their
suggestiveness, and consequently their reality, is
continually expanding. "I rest not from my
great task," he cries—

To open the eternal worlds, to open the immortal eyes
Of man inwards into the worlds of thought, into eternity,
Ever expanding in the bosom of God, the human imagination.

In Blake's view the qualities most sorely needed

by men are not restraint and discipline, obedience or a sense of duty, but love and understanding. " Men are admitted into heaven, not because they have curbed and governed their passions, or have no passions, but because they have cultivated their understandings." To understand is three parts of love, and it is only through Imagination that we *can* understand. It is the lack of imagination that is at the root of all the cruelties and all the selfishness in the world. Until we can feel for all that lives, Blake says in effect, until we can respond to the joys and sorrows of others as quickly as to our own, our imagination is dull and incomplete :

> Each outcry of the hunted Hare
> A fibre from the Brain does tear.
> A Skylark wounded in the wing
> A Cherubim does cease to sing.
>
> *Auguries of Innocence.*

When we feel like this, we will go forth to help, not because we are prompted by duty or religion or reason, but because the cry of the weak and ignorant so wrings our heart that we cannot leave it unanswered. Cultivate love and understanding then, and all else will follow. Energy, desire, intellect ; dangerous and deadly forces in the selfish and impure, become in the pure in heart the greatest forces for good. What mattered to Blake, and the only thing that mattered, was the

purity of his soul, the direction of his will or desire,
as Law and Boehme would have put it. Once a
man's desire is in the right direction, the more he
gratifies it the better ;

> Abstinence sows sand all over
> The ruddy limbs & flaming hair,
> But Desire Gratified
> Plants fruits of life & beauty there.[1]

Only an extraordinarily pure nature or a singularly
abandoned one could confidently proclaim such
a dangerous doctrine. But in Blake's creed, as
Swinburne has said, " the one thing unclean is
the belief in uncleanness."

It is easy to see that this faculty which Blake
calls " Imagination " entails of itself naturally and
inevitably the Christian doctrine of self-sacrifice.
It is in *Milton* that Blake most fully develops his
great dogma of the eternity of sacrifice. " One
must die for another through all eternity " ; only
thus can the bonds of " selfhood " be broken.
Milton, just before his renunciation, cries—

> I will go down to self-annihilation and eternal death
> Lest the Last Judgment come and find me unannihilate,
> And I be seiz'd and giv'n into the hands of my own Selfhood.

For, according to Blake, personal love or selfishness
is the one sin which defies redemption. This whole
passage in *Milton* (Book i., pp. 12, 13) well repays

[1] *Poems*, ed. Sampson, p. 173.

study, for one feels it to be alive with meaning,
holding symbol within symbol. Blake's symbolism,
and his fourfold view of nature and of man, is a
fascinating if sometimes a despairing study. Blake
has explained very carefully the way in which the
visionary faculty worked in him :—

> What to others a trifle appears
> Fills me full of smiles or tears ;
> For double the vision my Eyes do see,
> And a double vision is always with me.
> With my inward Eye, 'tis an old Man grey,
> With my outward, a Thistle across my way.
>
> .   .   .   .   .   .
>
> Now I a fourfold vision see,
> And a fourfold vision is given to me;
> 'Tis fourfold in my supreme delight,
> And threefold in soft Beulah's night,
> And twofold Always. May God us keep
> From Single vision & Newton's sleep! [1]

He says twofold always, for everything was of
value to Blake as a symbol, as a medium for expressing a still greater thing behind it. It was
in this way that he looked at the human body,
physical beauty, splendour of colour, insects, animals,
states, and emotions, male and female, contraction
and expansion, division and reunion, heaven and hell.

---

[1] *Poems*, ed. Sampson, pp. 305-6, 309-10. Blake is here praying
that we may be preserved from the condition of mind which sees
no farther than the concrete facts before it ; a condition he unfairly
associated with the scientific mind in the abstract, and more especially
with Newton.

When his imagination was at its strongest, his vision was fourfold, corresponding to the fourfold division of the Divine Nature, Father, Son, Spirit, and the fourth Principle, which may be described as the Imagination of God, without which manifestation would not be possible.[1] These principles, when condensed and limited so as to be seen by us, may take the form of Reason, Emotion, Energy and Sensation, or, to give them Boehme's names, Contraction, Expansion, Rotation, and Vegetative life. These, in turn, are associated with the four states of humanity or "atmospheres," the four elements, the four points of the compass, the four senses (taste and touch counting as one), and so on. Blake seemed, as it were, to hold his vision in his mind in solution, and to be able to condense it into gaseous, liquid, or solid elements at whatever point he willed. Thus we feel that the prophetic books contain meaning within meaning, bearing interpretation from many points of view ; and to arrive at their full value, we should need to be able—as Blake was—to apprehend all simultaneously,[2] instead

[1] This is the principle called occasionally by Blake, and always by Boehme, the " Mirror," or " Looking Glass." Blake's names for these four principles, as seen in the world, in contracted form, are Urizen, Luvah, Urthona, and Tharmas.

[2] Possibly in some such way as Mozart, when composing, heard the whole of a symphony. "Nor do I hear in my imagination the parts *successively*, but I hear them as it were all at once" (Holmes's *Life and Correspondence of Mozart,* 1845, pp. 317-18).

of being forced laboriously to trace them out one by one in succession. It is this very faculty of " fourfold vision " which gives to these books their ever-changing atmosphere of suggestion, elusive and magical as the clouds and colours in a sunset sky, which escape our grasp in the very effort to study them. Hence, for the majority even of imaginative people, who possess at the utmost " double vision," they are difficult and often wearisome to read. They are so, because the inner, living, vibrating ray or thread of connection which evokes these forms and beings in Blake's imagination, is to the ordinary man invisible and unfelt ; so that the quick leap of the seer's mind from figure to figure, and from picture to picture, seems irrational and obscure.

To this difficulty on the side of the reader, there must in fairness be added certain undeniable limitations on the part of the seer. These are principally owing to lack of training, and possibly to lack of patience, sometimes also it would seem to defective vision. So that his symbols are at times no longer true and living, but artificial and confused.

Blake has visions, though clouded and imperfect, of the clashing of systems, the birth and death of universes, the origin and meaning of good and evil, the function and secret correspondences of spirits, of states, of emotions, of passions, and of senses, as well as of all forms in earth and sky and sea.

This, and much more, he attempts to clothe in concrete forms or symbols, and if he fails at times to be explicit, it is conceivable that the fault may lie as much with our density as with his obscurity. Indeed, when we speak of Blake's obscurity, we are uncomfortably reminded of Crabb Robinson's naïve remark when recording Blake's admiration for Wordsworth's *Immortality Ode* : " The parts . . . which Blake most enjoyed were the most obscure—at all events, those which I least like and comprehend."

Blake's view of good and evil is the characteristically mystical one, in his case much emphasised. The really profound mystical thinker has no fear of evil, for he cannot exclude it from the one divine origin, else the world would be no longer a unity but a duality. This difficulty of " good " and " evil," the crux of all philosophy, has been approached by mystical thinkers in various ways (such as that evil is illusion, which seems to be Browning's view), but the boldest of them, and notably Blake and Boehme, have attacked the problem directly, and carrying mystical thought to its logical conclusion, have unhesitatingly asserted that God is the origin of Good and Evil alike, that God and the devil, in short, are but two sides of the same Force. We have seen how this is worked out by Boehme, and that the central point of his philosophy is that all manifestation necessitates opposition. In like manner, Blake's statement, "Without Contraries is no progression," is, in truth, the keynote to all his vision and mythology.

Attraction and Repulsion, Reason and Energy, Love and Hate, are necessary to Human existence.

From these contraries spring what the religious call Good and Evil.

Good is the passive that obeys Reason. Evil is the active springing from Energy. Good is Heaven. Evil is Hell.

With these startling remarks Blake opens what is the most intelligible and concise of all the prophetic books, *The Marriage of Heaven and Hell*. Swinburne calls it the greatest of Blake's books, and ranks it as about the greatest work " produced by the eighteenth century in the line of high poetry and spiritual speculation." We may think Swinburne's praise excessive, but at any rate it is well worth reading *(Essay on Blake*, 1906 edn., pp. 226-252). Certainly, if one work had to be selected as representative of Blake, as containing his most characteristic doctrines clothed in striking form, this is the book to be chosen. Place a copy of *The Marriage of Heaven and Hell* in the hands of any would-be Blake student (an original or facsimile copy, needless to say, containing Blake's exquisite designs, else the book is shorn of half its force and beauty) ; let him ponder it closely, and he will either be repelled and shocked, in which case he had better read no more Blake, or he will be strangely stirred and thrilled, he will be touched with a spark of the fire from Blake's spirit which quickens its words as the leaping tongues of flame illuminate its pages. The kernel of the book, and indeed of all Blake's message, is contained in the following statements on p. 4, headed " The Voice of the Devil."

All Bibles or sacred codes have been the causes of the following Errors :—

1. That man has two real existing principles, viz. a Body and a Soul.

2. That Energy, called Evil, is alone from the Body ; and that reason, called Good, is alone from the Soul.

3. That God will torment Man in Eternity for following his Energies.

But the following Contraries to these are True :—

1. Man has no Body distinct from his Soul, for that called Body is a portion of Soul discerned by the five Senses, the chief inlets of Soul in this age.

2. Energy is the only life and is from the Body, and Reason is the bound or outward circumference of Energy.

3. Energy is Eternal Delight.

Blake goes on to write down some of the Proverbs which he collected while walking among the fires of hell. These " Proverbs of Hell " fill four pages of the book, and they are among the most wonderful things Blake has written. Finished in expression, often little jewels of pure poetry, they are afire with thought and meaning, and inexhaustible in suggestion. Taken all together they express in epigrammatic form every important doctrine of Blake's. Some of them, to be fully understood, must be read in the light of his other work. Thus, " The road of excess leads to the palace of wisdom," or, " If the fool would persist in his folly he would become wise," are expressions of the idea constantly recurrent with Blake that evil must be embodied or experienced before it can be rejected.[1] But the greater number of them are quite clear and present no difficulty, as for instance the following :—

A fool sees not the same tree that a wise man sees.

He whose face gives no light shall never become a star.

No bird soars too high, if he soars with his own wings.

What is now proved was once only imagined.

As the air to a bird or the sea to a fish, so is contempt to the contemptible.

Exuberance is Beauty.

Everything possible to be believed is an image of truth.

There are two tendencies of Blake's mind, both mystical—that is, rooted in unity—the understanding of which helps, on the one hand, to clear much in

[1] Cf., for instance, " To be an error, and to be cast out, is a part of God's design " (A Vision of the Last Judgment, Gilchrist's Life, ii. p. 195); and Illustrations 2 and 16 to the Book of Job, see the commentary on them in Blake's Vision of the Book of Job, by J. H. Wicksteed, 1910, p. 21 and note 4. It is interesting to note that, as Mr Bradley points out (Shakesperian Tragedy, pp. 37, 39, 324, 325), it is a cognate idea which seems to underlie Shakesperian tragedy, and to make it bearable.

his writing that seems strange and difficult ; and, on the other, reveals a deep meaning in remarks apparently simple to the point of silliness. These are his view of the solidarity of mental and spiritual as compared with physical things, and his habit of concentrating a universal truth into some one small fact.

For Blake, mental and spiritual things are the only real things. Thought is more real than action, and spiritual attitude is more real than thought. It is the most real thing about us, and it is the only thing that is of any importance. The difference between Blake's attitude and that of the ordinary practical man of the world is summed up in his characteristic pencil comment in his copy of Bacon's *Essays* on the remark, " Good thoughts are little better than good dreams," in the Essay on Virtue. Blake writes beside this, " Thought *is* act." This view is well exemplified in the Job illustrations, where Blake makes quite clear his view of the worthlessness, spiritually, of Job's gift to the beggar of part of his last meal, because of the consciously meritorious attitude of Job's mind.[1]

If this attitude be remembered it explains a good many of the most startling and revolutionary views of Blake. For instance, in the poems called

[1] See the whole exposition of the Job illustrations by Wicksteed, and specially p. 37.

" Holy Thursday " in the *Songs of Innocence and Experience,* he paints first of all with infinite grace and tenderness the picture of the orphan charity children going to church, as it would appear to the ordinary onlooker.

> The hum of multitudes was there, but multitudes of lambs,
> Thousands of little boys & girls raising their innocent hands.
>
> . . . .
>
> Beneath them sit the aged men, wise guardians of the poor;
> Then cherish pity, lest you drive an angel from your door.

But in short, scathing words and significant change of metre he reverses the picture to show his view of it, when, in the companion song of " Experience," he asks—

> Is this a holy thing to see
> In a rich and fruitful land,
> Babes reduc'd to misery,
> Fed with cold and usurous hand ?

It is owing to a false idea that we can bear to see this so-called " charity " at all, for we—

> reduce the man to want a gift, and then give with pomp.

The real evil is that we can suffer the need of the crust of bread to exist. This is a view which is gradually beginning to be realised to-day.

Blake is peculiarly daring and original in his use of the mystical method of crystallising a great truth in an apparently trivial fact. We have seen some of these truths in the Proverbs, and the *Auguries of Innocence* is nothing else but a series of such facts, a storehouse of deepest wisdom. Some of these have the simplicity of nursery rhymes, they combine the direct freshness of the language of the child with the profound truth of the inspired seer.

> If the Sun & Moon should Doubt
> They'd immediately Go Out.

It would scarcely be possible to sum up more conpletely than does this artless couplet the faith—not only of Blake—but of every mystic. Simple, ardent, and living, their faith is in truth their life, and the veriest shadow of doubt would be to them a condition of death. They are the only people in the world who are the " possessors of certainty." They have seen, they have felt : what need they of further proof ? Logic, philosophy, theology, all alike are but empty sounds and barren forms to those who know.

To Francis Thompson the presence of the Divine in all things is the one overwhelming fact. As a result of this sense, the consciousness that everything is closely related, closely linked together, is ever present in his poetry. It is the vision of this truth, he believes, which will be the revelation of a new heaven and a new earth.

When to the new eyes of thee
All things by immortal power,
Near or far,
Hiddenly
To each other linkèd are,
That thou canst not stir a flower
Without troubling of a star.

The Mistress of Vision.

His " Divine intoxication," his certainty of the
presence of God, is the more remarkable when it is
realised through what depths of want and degradation and suffering Thompson passed, and what his
life was for many years.   His father, a north-country
doctor, wished him to follow the profession of
medicine, but the son could not bear it, and so he
ran away from home with—for sole wealth—a
Blake in one pocket and an Æschylus in the other.
In his struggle for life in London, fragile in body
and sensitive in soul, he sank lower and lower,
from selling boots to errand-boy, and finally for
five years living as a vagabond without home or
shelter, picking up a few pence by day, selling
matches or fetching cabs, and sleeping under the
archways of Covent Garden Market at night.   At
last, in the very depth of his misery, he was sought
out and rescued by the editor of the paper to
whom he had sent *Health and Holiness* and some
of his poems.   This saved him, his work brought
him good friends, and he was enabled to write
his wonderful poetry.   These terrible experiences,

which would have quenched the faith of the ordinary man and led him to despair, with the poet mystic sought expression in those six triumphant verses found among his papers when he died,[1] verses charged with mystic passion, which assert the solid reality of spiritual things, and tell us that to the outcast and the wanderer every place was holy ground, Charing Cross was the gate of heaven, and that he beheld—

> Christ walking on the water
> Not of Gennesareth, but Thames !

Through all that he writes there breathes the spirit of mystic devotion and aspiration, but the following characteristics and beliefs may be specially noted.

(1) His reverence of childhood. He sees in the child something of the divinity which Vaughan and Wordsworth saw, and his poems to children, such as *Daisy* and *The Poppy*, have a special quality of passionate worship all their own.

(2) His attitude towards the beauty of woman. This is entirely mystical, and is akin to the view of Plato and of Donne. He shares their belief that love is but the power to catch sight of the beauty of the soul, which shines through and actually moulds the beauty of face and body.

[1] *In no Strange Land.* Selected Poems, 1908, p. 130.

> How should I gauge what beauty is her dole,
> Who cannot see her countenance for her soul,
> As birds see not the casement for the sky ?
> And, as 'tis check they prove its presence by,
> I know not of her body till I find
> My flight debarred the heaven of her mind.

Her Portrait.

(3) His attraction towards the continual change and renewal of nature, not only of the movement of life to death, but of death to life. He broods over the changing cycles of the year, winter and spring, decay and re-birth, and he sees in them a profound and far-reaching symbolism. This is magnificently expressed in the *Ode to the Setting Sun*, where he paints a picture, unmatched in English verse, of the sun sinking to rest amid the splendours gathered round him in his fall. The poem is charged with mystic symbolism, the main thought of which is that human life, ending apparently in death, is but the prelude of preparation for a more glorious day of spiritual re-birth.

> For birth hath in itself the germ of death,
>   But death hath in itself the germ of birth.
> It is the falling acorn buds the tree,
> The falling rain that bears the greenery,
>   The fern-plants moulder when the ferns arise.
>   For there is nothing lives but something dies,
> And there is nothing dies but something lives.

But Francis Thompson's most entirely mystical utterance is the famous Ode—*The Hound of Heaven*

—where he pictures with a terrible vividness and in phrase of haunting music the old mystic idea of the Love chase.[1] It is the idea expressed by Plotinus when he says, " God . . . is present with all things, though they are ignorant that He is so. For they fly from Him, or rather from themselves. They are unable, therefore, to apprehend that from which they fly " (*Ennead*, vi. § 7). We see the spirit of man fleeing in terror " down the nights and down the days " before the persistent footsteps of his "tremendous Lover," until, beaten and exhausted, he finds himself at the end of the chase face to face with God, and he realises there is for him no escape and no hiding-place save in the arms of God Himself.

The voices of the English poets and writers form but one note in a mighty chorus of witnesses whose testimony it is impossible for any thoughtful person to ignore. Undoubtedly, in the case of some mystics, there has been great disturbance both of the psychic and physical nature, but on this account to disqualify the statements of Plotinus, St Augustine, Eckhart, Catherine of Siena, Catherine of Genoa, Blake, and Wordsworth, would seem analogous to Macaulay's view that " perhaps no person can be a poet, or

[1] For other examples of the expression of this idea of the " Following Love," the quest of the soul by God, especially in the anonymous Middle English poem of *Quia amore langueo*, see *Mysticism*, by Evelyn Underhill, pp. 158-162.

can even enjoy poetry without a certain unsoundness of mind." Our opinion about this must depend on what we mean by "soundness of mind." To some it may appear possible that the mystics and poets are as sound as their critics. In any case, the unprejudiced person to-day would seem driven to the conclusion that these people, who are, many of them, exceptionally great, intellectually and morally, are telling us of a genuine experience which has transformed life for them. What, then, is the meaning of this experience ? What explanation can we give of this puzzling and persistent factor in human life and history ? These are not easy questions to answer, and only a bare hint of lines of solution dare be offered.

It is of interest to note that the last word in science and philosophy tends to reinforce and even to explain the position of the mystic. The latest of European philosophers, M. Bergson, builds up on a mystical basis the whole of his method of thought, that is, on his perception of the simple fact that true duration, the real time-flow, is known to us by a state of feeling which he calls intuition, and not by an intellectual act.

He says something like this. We find as a matter of practice that certain problems when presented to the intellect are difficult and even impossible to solve, whereas when presented to our experience of life, their solution is so obvious that they cease to be problems. Thus, the unaided intellect might be puzzled to say how sounds can grow more alike by continuing to grow more different. Yet a child can answer the question by sounding an octave on the piano. But this solution is reached by having sensible knowledge of the reality and not by logical argument. Bergson's view, therefore, is that the intellect has been evolved for practical purposes, to deal in a certain way with material things by cutting up into little bits what is an undivided flow of movement, and by looking at these little bits side by side, This, though necessary for practical life, is utterly misleading when we assume that the " points " thus singled out by the intellect represent the " thickness " of reality. Reality is fluidity, and we cannot dip up its substance with the intellect which deals with surfaces, even as we cannot dip up water with a net, however finely meshed. Reality is movement, and movement is the one thing we are unable intellectually to realise.

In order to grasp reality we must use the faculty of contact or immediate feeling, or, as Bergson calls it, intuition. Intuition is a different order of knowledge, it is moulded on the very form of life, and it enables us to enter into life, to be one with it, to live it. It is " a direction of movement : and, although capable of infinite development, is simplicity itself." This is the mystic art, which in its early stages is a direction of movement, an alteration of the quality and intensity of the self. So Bergson, making use of and applying the whole range of modern psychology and biology, tells us that we must develop intuition as a philo-sophical instrument if we are to gain any knowledge of things in themselves ; and he is thus re-echoing in modern terms what was long ago stated by Plotinus when he said—

Knowledge has three degrees — opinion, science, illumination. The means or instrument of the first is sense, of the second dialectic, of the third intuition. To the last I subordinate reason. It is absolute knowledge founded on the identity of the mind knowing with the object known. (*Letter to Flaccus.*)

We have discovered that sense knowledge, how-ever acute, has to be corrected by the intellect, which tells us that the sun does not go round the earth, although it appears to our observation to do this. So possibly, in turn, the intellect, however acute, may have to be corrected by intuition, and the impotence of brain knowledge in dealing with the problem of life is leading slowly to the perception that to *know* in its true sense is not an intellectual process at all.

Further, in Bergson's theory of the nature of mind, and in his theory of rhythm, he seems to indicate the lines of a technical explanation of some part of the mystic experience.[1] The soul, or the total psychic and mental life of man, he says, is far greater than the little bit of consciousness of which we are normally aware, and the brain acts as a sheath or screen, which allows only a point of this mental life to touch reality. The brain or the cerebral life is therefore to the whole mental life as the point of a knife is to the knife itself. It limits the field of vision, it cuts in one direction only, it puts blinkers on the mind, forcing it to concentrate on a limited range of facts. It is conceivable that what happens with the mystics is that their mental blinkers become slightly shifted, and they are thus able to respond to another aspect or order of reality. So that they are swept by emotions and invaded by harmonies from which the average man is screened. Life having for them somewhat changed in direction, the brain is forced to learn new movements, to cut along fresh channels, and thus to receive sensations which do not directly minister to the needs of physical life. " Our knowledge of things," says Bergson, " derives its form from our bodily functions and lower needs. By unmaking that which these needs have made, we

[1] The following remarks are much indebted to a valuable article on *Bergson and the Mystics*, by Evelyn Underhill, in the *English Review*, Feb. 1912, which should be consulted for a fuller exposition of the light shed by Bergson's theories on the mystic experience.

may restore to Intuition its original purity, and
so recover contact with the Real." It is possibly
this very unmaking and remaking, this readjust-
ment, which we see at work in the lives of the great
mystics, and which naturally causes great psychic
and even physical disturbances.

Bergson's theory of rhythm is peculiarly illuminating in this connection. The intellect, he says,
is like a cinematograph. Moving at a certain pace,
it takes certain views, snapshots of the continuous
flux of reality, of which it is itself a moving part. The
special views that it picks out and registers, depend
entirely upon the relation between its movement
and the rhythm or movement of other aspects of
the flux. It is obvious that there are a variety of
rhythms or tensions of duration. For example,
in what is the fraction of a second of our own
duration, hundreds of millions of vibrations, which
it would need thousands of our years to count,
are taking place successively in matter, and giving
us the sensation of light. It is therefore clear
that there is a great difference between the
rhythm of our own duration and the incredibly
rapid rhythms of physical matter. If an alteration
took place in our rhythm, these same physical
movements would make us conscious—not of light—
but of some other thing quite unknown.

" Would not the whole of history," asks Bergson,

" be contained in a very short time for a consciousness at a higher degree of tension than our own ? "
A momentary quickening of rhythm might thus
account for the sensation of timelessness, of the
" participation in Eternity " so often described by
the mystic as a part of the Vision of God.

Again, Bergson points out that there is nothing
but movement ; that the idea of *rest* is an illusion,
produced when we and the thing we are looking at
are moving at the same speed, as when two railway
trains run side by side in the same direction. Here,
once more, may not the mystic sensation of " stillness," of being at one with the central Life, be
owing to some change having taken place in the
spiritual rhythm of the seer, approximating it to
that of the Reality which he is thus enabled to
perceive, so that the fretful movement of the
individual mind becomes merged in the wider
flow of the whole, and both seem to be at rest ?

Thus, the most recent philosophy throws light
on the most ancient mystic teaching, and both
point to the conclusion that our normal waking
consciousness is but one special type of many other
forms of consciousness, by which we are surrounded,
but from which we are, most of us, physically
and psychically screened. We know that the
consciousness of the individual self was a late
development in the race ; it is at least possible that

the attainment of the consciousness that this individual self forms part of a larger Whole, may prove
to be yet another step forward in the evolution of the
human spirit. If this be so, the mystics would appear
to be those who, living with an intensity greater than
their fellows, are thus enabled to catch the first
gleams of the realisation of a greater self. In any
case, it would seem certain, judging from their
testimony, that it is possible, by applying a certain
stimulus, to gain knowledge of another order of
consciousness of a rare and vivifying quality. Those
who have attained to this knowledge all record that
it must be felt to be understood, but that, so far
as words are of use, it is ever of the nature of a
reconciliation ; of discord blending into harmony,
of difference merging into unity.

BIBLIOGRAPHY

NOTE.—The literature on mysticism is growing very large, and the following is only a small selection from the general works on it. In the case of individual writers, references are given only where there might be difficulty about editions. Thus no references are given to the works of Burke, Carlyle, Wordsworth, Shelley, Tennyson, Browning, etc.

GENERAL

Underhill, Evelyn. *Mysticism*, Methuen, 1911. (See the valuable Bibliography of mystical works, pp. 563-585.)
> *The Mystic Way*, Dent, 1913.

Jones, Rufus M. *Studies in Mystical Religion*, Macmillan, 1909.

James, William. *The Varieties of Religious Experience*, Longmans Green, 1905.

Inge, W. R. *Christian Mysticism*, Methuen, 1899.
> *Studies of English Mystics*, Murray, 1905.
> *Light, Life and Love.* Selections from the German mystics. With Introduction. Methuen, 1904.

Hügel, Baron F. von. *The Mystical Element in Religion*, 2 vols., Dent, 1909.

Delacroix, H. *Études d'Histoire et de Psychologie du Mysticisme*, Paris, 1908.

Récéjac, E. *Essai sur les fondements de la Connaissance Mystique*, Paris, 1897 (translated by S. C. Upton, London, 1899).

Gregory, Eleanor C. *A Little Book of Heavenly Wisdom.* Selections from some English prose mystics, with Introduction. Methuen, 1902.

FOREIGN INFLUENCES

Plato (*c.* 427-347 B.C.). *Opera*, ed. J. Burnet, 5 vols. (Bibliotheca Scriptorum Classicorum Oxoniensis), 1899-1907.

Plato (Eng. trans.) *The Dialogues*, translated by B. Jowett, 5 vols., Oxford, 3rd ed., 1892.

Plotinus (A.D. 204-270). *Plotini Enneades, præmisso Porphyrii de vita Plotini deque ordine librorum ejus libello*, edidit R. Volkmann, 2 vols., Leipzig, 1883-84.

(Eng. trans.) There is no complete English translation of the *Enneads*, only *Select Works*, translated by T. Taylor, 1817 ; re-issued, George Bell, 1895.

(French trans.) *Les Ennéades de Plotin*, translated by M.-N. Bouillet, 3 vols., Paris, 1857-61. (This is complete and very good, but out of print.)

The best critical account of Plotinus is in *The Evolution of Theology in the Greek Philosophers*, by Edward Caird, 2 vols., Maclehose, 1904.

Dionysius the Areopagite. *Works*, translated Parker, 1897.

Jacob Boehme (1575-1624). *Works* (incomplete), 4 vols., 1764-81. Reprint of complete works in progress, ed. C. J. Barker, published J. Watkins. (See Bibliography to chap. xii. of *Cambridge History of English Literature*, vol. ix.)

Emmanuel Swedenborg (1688-1772). *Works*, published by the Swedenborg Society, London. Selections, *A Compendium of the Theological Writings*, ed. Warren, 1901.

ENGLISH WRITERS

Thomas de Hales (fl. 1250). *A Luve Ron*, (printed in) Morris's Old English Miscellany (E.E.T.S.), 1872.

Richard Rolle (1290 ? - 1349). *Richard Rolle and his Followers*, ed. Horstmann, 2 vols., Sonnenschein, 1895-6.

The Fire of Love, and the Mending of Life, ed. R. Harvey (E.E.T.S.), 1896.

Anonymous (*c.* 1350-1400). *The Cloud of Unknowing*, ed. Evelyn Underhill, J. Watkins, 1912.

The Epistle of Prayer
The Epistle of Discretion
The Treatise of Discerning Spirits
} All printed, with other early English mystical treatises, in *The Cell of Self-Knowledge*, ed. E. G. Gardner, Chatto & Windus, 1910.

Anonymous. *The Epistle of Privy Counsel*, in MS., British Museum, Harleian, 674 and 2473.

(William Langland, or other authors. ? *c.* 1362-1399). *The Vision of William Concerning Piers the Plowman*, ed. Skeat, 2 vols., Oxford, 1886.

    Jusserand, J. J. *Piers Plowman: a Contribution to the History of English Mysticism*. Translated from the French by M. E. R., 1894.

Walter Hylton (d. 1396). *The Scale of Perfection*, ed. Guy, 1869; ed. Dalgairns, 1870.

    The Song of Angels, printed by Gardner, in *The Cell of Self-Knowledge*, 1910.

Julian of Norwich (1342-1413 ?). *Revelations of Divine Love*, ed. Warrack, Methuen, 1912.

Richard Crashaw (1613 ?-1649). *Poems*, ed. A. R. Waller, Cambridge, 1904.

John Donne (1573-1631). *Poetical Works*, ed. Grierson, 2 vols., Oxford, 1912.

George Herbert (1593-1633). *Poems*, ed. Grosart, 1891; Oxford edition, 1907.

Christopher Harvey (1597-1663). *Poems*, ed. Grosart, 1874.

Henry More (1614-1687). *Complete Poems*, ed. Grosart, 1878.

Life, by R. Ward, 1710, reprinted Theosophical Society, ed. Howard, 1911.

Henry Vaughan (1622-1695). *Poems*, ed. Chambers, 2 vols., 1896.

Thomas Traherne (*c.* 1636-1674). *Poetical Works*, ed. Dobell, 1903.
    Centuries of Meditations, ed. Dobell, 1908.
    Poems of Felicity, ed. Bell, Oxford, 1910.

William Law (1686-1761). *Works*, 9 vols., 1753-76, reprinted privately by G. Moreton, 1892-3.

    The Liberal and Mystical Writings of William Law, ed. W Scott Palmer, 1908.

    (See Bibliography to chap xii. of *Cambridge History of English Literature*, vol. ix., 1912.)

William Blake (1757-1827). *Works*, ed. Ellis and Yeats, 3 vols., Quaritch, 1893.

William Blake. *Poetical Works* (including Prophetic Books), ed, Ellis, 2 vols., Chatto and Windus, 1906.

Poetical Works (exclusive of Prophetic Books), ed. Sampson, Oxford, 1905. (The best text of the poems.)

Life, by Gilchrist, 2 vols., Macmillan, 1880.

William Blake, by A. C. Swinburne, Chatto and Windus (new ed.), 1906.

William Blake, Mysticisme et Poésie, par P. Berger, Paris, 1907.

S. T. Coleridge (1772-1834). *Complete Poetical Works*, ed. E. H. Coleridge, 2 vols., Oxford, 1912.

Biographia Literaria, ed. J. Shawcross, 2 vols., Oxford, 1907.

Emily Brontë (1818-1848). *Complete Poems*, ed. Shorter, Hodder and Stoughton, 1910.

The Three Brontës, by May Sinclair, Hutchinson, 1912.

Coventry Patmore (1823-1896). *Poems*, G. Bell, 1906.

The Rod, the Root, and the Flower, 1895.

Memoirs and Correspondence of C. Patmore, by B. Champneys, 1900.

Richard Jefferies (1848-1887). *The Story of my Heart*, 1883, (reprinted) Longmans, 1907.

Francis Thompson (1859-1907). *New Poems*, Burns and Oates, 1897.

Selected Poems, 1908.

Sister Songs, 1908.

INDEX

Æschylus, 148

Alchemists, 57

Allen, H. E., *Authorship of the Prick of Conscience*, 120

Ammonius Sakkas, 17

Ancren Riwle, 115

Bacon, Francis, *Essays*, 145

Beauty, 22, 46, 47, 60, 76 ; moon the symbol of, 54 ; Plato on, 47, 149 ; truth and, 32, 55 ; worship of, 77

Behmenists, 88, 89. (*See* also under Boehme)

Bergson, mystical basis of his thought, 152 ; study of, 152-8 ; theory of rhythm, 154

Bhagavad-Gîtâ, 3

Blake, William, 111, 151 ; *Auguries of Innocence*, 147 ; *Europe*, 134-5 ; *Everlasting Gospel*, 132 ; Illustrations to *Job*, 144, 145 ; imagination of, 14, 28, 36, 135, 140, 142 ; indebtedness to Boehme, 28 ; greatness of, 111, 129 ; *Marriage of Heaven and Hell*, 78, 83, 142-3 ; *Milton*, 131, 137 ; *Of Natural Religion*, 133 ; *Songs of Innocence*, 131, 146 ; study of, 129-147 ; view of Nature, 2 ; *Vision of Last Judgment*, 144

Boehme, Jacob, 14, 62, 131, 137 ;

Coleridge on, 31 ; influence of, 32, 49, 89, 91-3 ; Law's use of, 28, 91-6 ; study of, 91-3 ; view of evil, 141

Bourignon, Madame, 89, 91

Bradley, A. C., *Shakespearian Tragedy*, 144

Brontë, Charlotte, 81

—— Emily, 72 ; *Last Lines*, 83-4 ; *Philosopher*, 83 ; *Prisoner*, 82 ; study of, 80-4 ; *Visionary*, 83

Browne, Sir Thomas, 76

Browning, Elizabeth Barrett, 32 ; *Aurora Leigh*, 30, 31

Browning, Robert, 12, 14, 15, 46, 72, 110 ; *Asolando*, 43 ; *Beanstripe*, 43 ; his central teaching, 41 ; *Death in the Desert*, 40 ; his intellectuality, 35 ; his love-mysticism, 33-4, 40-3 ; *Paracelsus*, 40, 45 ; on pre-existence, 44 ; *Prince Hohenstiel-Schwangau*, 39 ; *Rabbi ben Ezra*, 40 ; on religion and science, 40 ; resemblance to Eckhart, 41-3 ; *Ring and the Book*, 40, 45, 46 ; *Statue and Bust*, 43 ; study of, 38-46 ; his view of evil, 141

Bruno, Giordano, 2

Bunyan, John, 27

Burke, Edmund, 32, 56, 72, 88 ; *Present Discontents*, 102 ; study of, 100-2

Byron, 13

163